A STRANGE PATH TO POWER

by Dr. H. Beecher Hicks, Jr.

Urban Ministries, Inc.
Chicago, IL

Publisher
Urban Ministries, Inc.
P.O. Box 463987
Chicago, IL 60643-6987

ISBN: 0-940955-42-3

Scripture Quotations
Unless otherwise noted, Scripture texts are taken from the King
James Version (KJV) of the Bible.

DEDICATION

In recognition of our 20 years as Pastor and people, we hereby dedicate the royalties from *A Strange Path to Power* to the creation of the Metropolitan Day School, a legacy of Vision: 2000.

Dr. and Mrs. H. Beecher Hicks, Jr.

For Kristin, my special joy.

ACKNOWLEDGMENTS

This book could not have been completed without the diligent and skilled editorial review given by Ms. Sharlynn E. Bobo. For her labor I am profoundly grateful. I am also deeply indebted to Mrs. Barbara Barnes, Mrs. Carol Minick, and Mrs. Andrea Kittrell for their technical assistance in the production of this work.

Dr. H. Beecher Hicks, Jr.

TABLE OF CONTENTS

Introduction

A preacher is customarily found in the church pulpit on Sunday morning, delivering a sermon designed specifically for a given congregation. However, as the leader of the only existing institution indigenous to the African American community, the black preacher has an opportunity available to only a few. He or she is often called upon to speak on other occasions in a variety of settings, such as providing the invocation or benediction for a public event, blessing the dedication of new building or venture, making a speech for a public or private celebration, and delivering the eulogy for the memorial service of a public figure. The black preacher is also often called upon to represent the views of African Americans on issues of public discussion, especially in the arenas of public policy and political conduct.

As a preacher of the Gospel for more than 35 years, I have been blessed to share the Good News throughout the world. I have spoken the Word of the Lord in pulpits large and small, in banquet halls, public buildings, on television, at universities and on Capitol Hill. I have prayed, preached, spoken, admonished, cajoled, comforted and challenged. But my message is always the same: no matter where I am or who I'm talking to, I have only one topic—that the salvation of the world lies in the redemptive grace of Jesus Christ, the son of God.

Because of the era in which I matured as a preacher, I have always been sensitive to the social dimensions of the Gospel. Never one to remain silent in times of controversy, or to shy away from sensitive political issues, my goal has always been to ensure that my preaching was grounded in "real world" theology, believing that authentic preaching comes from the Bible and the newspaper. Metropolitan is the church where more than half of this preaching has been proclaimed; Washington, D.C. is the civic context within which I have ministered and preached. I have been blessed by generous support from both.

A Strange Path to Power is published on the anniversary of my 20 years in the pastorate of the Metropolitan Church. While the anniversary celebrates the journey of Pastor and people, it also affords me an opportunity to acknowledge the model for ministry which my father, Dr. H. Beecher Hicks, Sr., has provided for me and countless other preachers across America.

From the moment of my "call" in 1961, there's never been any doubt in my mind that the purpose for my being was to preach the gospel of Jesus Christ. Preaching in the African American community has served as the basis for my intellectual inquiry and the arena of my daily praxis. As an art form, preaching is never precise, nor can it be scientifically examined or philosophically defined. Preaching is an engagement of the human in the exercise of the divine. The words you find here are feeble at best. They represent, however, my sincere effort to be faithful to the anointment and the "call" which God has placed on my life.

This volume is a compendium of my public speaking and writing over the years. Included are sermons written and preached for three of the four churches I have pastored over the last 30 years: the Mt. Ararat Baptist Church in Pittsburgh, Pennsylvania, Antioch Missionary Baptist Church in Houston, Texas and the Metropolitan Baptist Church in Washington, D.C. The addresses include two given at universities from which my sons, H. Beecher Hicks III and the Reverend Ivan Douglas Hicks, received degrees, and an address given at a recent conference on Black Philanthropy. Two eulogies for the late Secretary of Commerce Ron Brown and D.C. City Council Chairperson, David Clarke; and prayers offered at the dedication of the new headquarters of the National Council for Negro Women (NCNW) and a TransAfrica Forum Dinner are here as well. Only two pieces, "From These Ashes," and "Give Me Liberty!," both editorials published in the Washington Post, were originally intended to be read rather than heard. The speech "Challenge to the African American Church: Problems and Perspectives for the Third Millennium," was published in the *Journal of Religious Thought* of Howard University following its delivery. "Testimony on Bill 12-280" was offered in opposition to a proposal for establishing the death penalty for persons convicted of killing law enforcement officers.

During this time of celebration of my Twentieth Anniversary Jubilee at Metropolitan, I thank God and His people for the privilege of spreading His Word.

❧ I ❧
Sermons

CHAPTER ONE

What Mean
These Stones?

ঔৣৣ৾ঌ

Mount Ararat Baptist Church
The first sermon preached in the new sanctuary
on Sunday, February 6, 1972.

I know what David meant. I can sense what he sensed. I experience what he experienced when he said:

One thing have I desired of the Lord, that will I seek after, that I may dwell in the house of the Lord all the days of my life, to behold the beauty of the Lord and to inquire in his temple. (Psalm 27:4)

It is good for us to be here. This is a high moment for the church. Last June when the church set its course in this direction we could not imagine the splendor of this hour. We could not dream of the majesty of this moment. But, here we are. Bloody but unbowed. Here we are. Not limping but leaping. Here we are. Tired but not intimidated. And if anybody asks you who we are and from whence we have come tell them:

These are they who have come up out of great tribulation and who have washed their robes white in the blood of the lamb. (Revelation 7:14).

I don't know how you feel about it but somebody ought to say, "thank you, Jesus. I thank you, Lord." For He brought us; yes, He brought us from a mighty, mighty long way. And it's good for us to be here.

Share with me now in these next few moments these words taken from the Book of Joshua 4:4-6 (NRSV):

Then Joshua called the twelve men from the people of Israel, whom he had appointed, a man from each tribe: and Joshua said to them, Pass on before the ark of the Lord your God into the midst of the Jordan, and take up each of you a stone upon his shoulder, according to the number of the tribes of the people of Israel, that this may be a sign among you, when your children ask in time to come, What mean these stones?

The Exodus was nearly over. Israel at last would receive the promise. This was the day for which Israel prayed and waited. The day when she would leave the land of wandering and come to the promised land of milk and honey.

Joshua was the leader. And Joshua had communed with God. God told Joshua to get the twelve tribes of Israel and for each to take a stone from the bed of the Jordan and place it on the other side of the Jordan. Joshua was told to take the stones and place them together in preparation for the time when posterity would ponder—*What mean these stones?*

We are living in a time when the question has become contemporary. The Church of Christ is under consistent query and insistent investigation. Men are concerned about the meaning of the church in our time and indeed, in any time. A few days ago I stood in Greece and saw etched across the skies the shadow of the Parthenon and the Acropolis—symbols of Grecian glory and the religious philosophies of man. Ruin and rubble now—and I asked myself: *What mean these stones?* I stood in the center of West Berlin and looked at a church bombed and gutted in World War II, but left there as a symbol of a decaying world, a degenerate society and perhaps a dying church. And I asked, *What mean these stones?* Over and over the critics of Christianity are challenging the institutional church, declaring that the church in modern times is through. And they too would ask, *What mean these stones?*

And the critics may be right. Somehow the church must give account for herself. The world is filled with churches great and small, splendid and simple, urban and suburban. For all their beauty the world still wants to know, *What mean these stones?*

The lesson of history is plain. The stones have no meaning; buildings have no meaning, churches have no meaning of themselves. There must be a meaning, a significance beyond the stones.

Israel had a great experience at the Jordan. It was a time for celebration, hand shaking and backslapping all around. God gave the order for the stones to be erected but with the reminder that someday, somebody, sometime would ask Israel the penetrating question, *What mean these stones?*

There is something significant about those stones. The stones in that day represented a testimony to the activity of God—not a vague sentimentality or a pious and meaningless demonstration of pride. God was saying something in the stones. God spoke to Israel through Joshua: Don't forget where you come from. Only yesterday there was no bread for your hunger and no water for your thirst. Don't forget. Only yesterday you were humiliated by bondage and scourged by slavery. Don't forget. Only yesterday you couldn't see for the tears that welled in your eyes and the anguish that tormented your heart. Don't forget.

You made a great getaway from Pharaoh, but I showed you how. Don't forget. You made it across the wilderness, but I gave you manna, milk and honey. Don't forget. You made it across the red sea on dry land, but don't forget I held back the rushing of the waters and made the way clear for you. Don't forget. You're in the promised land now, but don't forget how you got there!

What mean these stones? God knew that Israel would be quick to assume a posture of comfort and confidence. It did not take long to become accustomed to the prosperity of the promised land. Israel looked around and became pleased with her new circumstance. Somebody said, "We sure planned this thing well." Somebody said, "Moses knew what he was talking about, after all." Someone else may have said, "Joshua was a fine pastor. Look at what Rev. Joshua has done for us." But the stones speak of God and not of man. The stones don't have anything to do with Israel's Board of Trustees. The stones say, "God did it."

The preacher, the pastor always stands in the trying tension of wanting to boast and daring not to. Moses had to learn that lesson and so never saw the promised land. Joshua had to learn, too, that he was but the instrument of God and not God Himself. The preacher cannot afford to think to highly of himself. God is still in charge here. I must decrease that He might increase.

God told Joshua, "Don't you go first but send the ark of the covenant on ahead." The ark is where God dwelled and as long as

God was ahead, everything would be all right. God's got to be in front of the church or he that buildeth does so in vain. We need to let God lead. We need to let God get inside these walls. We need to let God into this church. We need to let God be the pastor, and that's all right with me.

But *What mean these stones?* The other day I saw in my library a book titled *The Last Days of the Church.* And I thought how in every age there has been an author for that book. Some say the church is clutching with futility to its last gasps of air. But the church survives. In spite of persecution and principalities, the church survives. In spite of the catacombs, the church survives. In spite of the dark ages, the church survives. In spite of the wars and rumors of wars, still the church survives. In spite of criticism on the outside and confusion on the inside the church survives. Somehow the old ship of Zion keeps on moving in the murky and muddy waters of this world and the gates of hell cannot prevail against it.

What has happened is that so many people have said so many negative things about the church until people in the church began to believe it themselves. If folk keep on telling you you're sick after awhile you get a headache. And you start believing you're really sick. But I'm satisfied that the church is not nearly as sick as the world would have us believe. There's something left here. There's something alive here. There's something moving right here. The church cannot afford to be deluded by this talk of sickness. "Take up your bed and walk." (Matthew 9:6) The church can't be lulled to sleep nor permitted to lie in lethargy. "Awake, awake, put on my strength, O Zion." (Isaiah 52:1)

The challenge is before us. For it won't do to just be beautiful. Mount Ararat can become so enamored with her beauty that she will sit right here and die a beautiful death.

This must be the place where the people of God unite to worship and depart to serve. This must be the place where the saints of God do battle against the harbors of hatred and pockets of poverty. It won't do to just sit and be pretty. We've got to do something to earn the right to be called the church of the living God. Too many people are dying, too many are cold, too many are unwanted, too many are unloved. We've got a job to do. This is the launching site, not the landing pad.

Those stones said something about life. Israel was tired. They had been marching for a long time in that wilderness. Hungry, tired, short-tempered, losing faith, up, down, and after forty years it seemed that they were no better off than they were when they started out. You remember, they started out at the water, they started out at the Red Sea. And now, after years of heartbreak, where are they? At the water.

There's something in that for us. I declare it looks like Black folk have been in the wilderness a long time. We've been searching for justice a long time. We've been searching for a way out to freedom a long time. And after 300 years of searching in this American wilderness, we're right back where we started. And you get tired sometimes. It gets hard sometimes. But the experience of Israel says to us: Keep on marching. Yes, we're lost, but keep on marching; Yes, we're tired, but keep on marching; Yes, we're disorganized, but keep on marching; Yes, we're worn out with the struggle, but keep on marching! Poor, on welfare, but keep on marching. You must make up your mind to cross the Jordan. Nobody's going to do anything for you. Moses can lead you. Joshua can lead you. But you must cross it for yourself.

Israel, you see, found out something after those long years of wandering. She found out that when they got to the water God was already there. You can't avoid the water in your life. You'll be met by the water of opposition and defeat. You'll be assaulted by the *water* of hatred and disdain. You'll be intimidated by the rising tide of trouble on every hand. But don't forget God made you and He made the water, too. The water says, I'm too wide and you can't cross. But God says, I'll make a way out of no way. The water says, You'll be drowned by the lashing of my waves. But God says, When thou passeth through the waters I'll be with you. The water says, My waters are too deep and my currents are too rapid. But God says, I'm a bridge over troubled waters. God will meet you at the water.

Biblical history says that when the children of Israel got to the promised land two and a half of the tribes elected not to go further into the promised land, but to stay with their cattle in the rich pastures of Gilead and Bashan. In other words, you can take some folk to the land and they still won't want to go. Give some folk a one way ticket to heaven and they'd still rather live at the gates of hell. You can beautify a sanctuary to the approval of heaven and somebody will still say, "I like it better the way it used to be." But don't worry about that. Your job is to just march. God will meet you at the water.

What mean these stones? Joshua was told by God to tell men that one day God dried up the Red Sea and the people passed by on dry ground. Tell men that the Lord is a mighty God. Tell men that God still determines our destiny.

But it is not enough to glory in an Old Exodus. And it's not enough to be satisfied with an old crossing of the chilly Jordan. If the stones of the church would have meaning there must be a new exodus and a new march. On this new march...

We will love one another like Christians ought.
We will leave strife behind and forget past deeds.
We will fight for justice against the pharoahs of this land.
We will "lift every voice and sing till earth and heaven ring, ring with the harmonies of liberty."
We will work for the kingdom of God to come on earth as it is in heaven.
We will let our light shine that men may glorify our Father.
We will leave the dusty roads of degradation and march up the king's highway.

We will tell the world about a man named Jesus.
I'm going to tell the world that Jesus is a way maker, Jesus is a heart fixer.
Jesus is the church's one foundation. Jesus is the tried stone of eternity. Jesus is the precious cornerstone.

Jesus is the world to me, my life, my joy, my all.
He is my strength from day to day, without Him I would fall.
Eternal life with such a friend. Eternal life, that has no end,
eternal life, eternal joy. He's my Friend.[1]

Well I don't know about you, but I'm glad that they crossed that Jordan. I'm so glad they made it to the other side. I'm so glad they set up stones of mercy; they set up stones of goodness; they set up stones of eternal love; they set up stones of amazing grace; they set up stones of soul salvation; they set up stones of redemption for the

[1] Will L. Thompson "Jesus Is All The World To Me," *Gospel Pearls* Nashville, TN: Sunday School Publishing Board, 1921. p. 51

righteous; they set up stones of justification; they set up stones of sanctification; they set up stones of truth; they set up stones of justice; they set up stones of brotherhood, to help me on my way.

And church, I haven't made it yet, you haven't made it yet, we haven't made it yet. But I'm on my way, yes I am.

On Jordan's stormy banks I stand
And cast a wishful eye
To Canaan's fair and happy land
where my possessions lie.
I am bound for the Promised Land
Oh, who will come and go with me?
I am bound for the Promised Land.[2]

---

[6] Stennett, Samuel. "On Jordan's Stormy Banks," *Baptist Standard Hymnal* Nashville, TN: Townsend Press, 1961. p. 581

CHAPTER TWO

Why Does A Caged Bird Sing?

✿

Antioch Missionary Baptist Church of Christ
Houston, Texas
1976

*H*ow shall we sing the Lord's song in a strange land? (Psalm 137:4)

I have often wondered why a caged bird sings. The thought intrigues me. How is it that this creature, who by nature glides from tree to tree and floats in leisurely comfort in the clouds, can still sing in a cage? How is it that this creature of God, endowed with wings to soar above the plane of men, can still find the resources to sing even when confined to man's level? How is it that even when its cage is small and its food is stale and its water is tepid and it is forced to stay confined and alone—why does a caged bird sing?

A long time ago the children of Israel were defeated in battle, demoralized by the plunder and ravage of war, and caught and caged like birds. There—I see them on the banks of the river of Babylon and the oppressor said, "Sing us one of Zion's Songs." I hear them saying, "This is not the way God intended it to be. We were not destined to live this way. God's people are supposed to be free people. We can't sing in this Babylonian cage."

The time has changed but the cage is still the same. Here we are between the shores of the Atlantic and the Pacific, caged by an unresponsive society, caged by a social order that burdens the poor and ignores the maimed. We are comforted by the promise of democracy, but we are caged by the denial of it. We are comforted by the promise of justice but we are caged by the inadequacy of it. How can we sing in the midst of oppression? How can we sing in the midst of injustice? How can we sing in the face of racism? How can we sing in the face of poverty? How can we sing the songs of Zion in a strange land? Why does a caged bird sing?

One cannot look at a caged bird and not realize that something is wrong with him. The most astonished people in the world were those Babylonians when Israel wouldn't sing. I hear someone saying: "I wonder why they don't sing? We treat them well. We give them food stamps twice a month. Why are they so violent? I heard they were happy religious people. Why don't they sing one of their songs? I just love to hear those people sing." It always amazes me how the world can look at people in bondage and chains and still want to know why they don't sing anymore.

A bird in a cage can never really spread his wings. A bird in a cage can never roam the forests in search of a mate. A bird in a cage will never really know what kind of bird God intended him to be. A bird in a cage will never smell the free fresh air of God's unpolluted wilderness. So I just don't understand why a caged bird would sing.

Basically, what's wrong with the caged bird is that he is not really free. You can build him a high rise cage but as long as he can't get out of the cage he's not free. You can clean up, fix up, and paint up all the cages but as long as he can't get out of the cage he's still not free. You can even put him in charge of the cage, give him community control of the cage, but if he can't get out of the cage he's still not free! The fact is that everybody wants to be free. One writer[3] speaks of the freedom for which man yearns—a freedom akin to that of wild animals which roam the forests and the fields. *Born free, as free as the wind blows, as free as the grass grows, born free to follow your heart.* No one wants to be cooped up, caught or bound. The human animal rebels at the thought of confinement or separation—no man is an island, no man wants to be shut off from the main. Claustrophobia is the psychological refusal of the spirit to be closed in by any environmental force. Man was meant to be free.

In our day there is a need for freedom. Not a literary freedom, nor a legislated freedom, but a freedom that is human and humane. We need personal freedom. The ability to be who we want to be and all that we can be and to be accepted by the world for who we are. Too often we let the world talk us out of what we want by making us believe that we are less than we are.

---

[3] Barry, John (music) Black, Don (lyrics) 1966 "Born Free," (song) fr. Screen Gems Columbia Pictures release "Born Free" (1967)

Surely we need social freedom in our land. No one can live in these times and not be caught up in the quest for social freedom and justice. We have rediscovered our pride and are willing to die for the freedom we seek. Those old words have been given new meaning in our time: *Before I'll be a slave, I'll be buried in my grave and go home to my Lord and be free.*

Not to be forgotten is the quest for spiritual freedom. All across our land the cry has gone out for worship to become celebration. New forms of worship are being introduced into our churches in an effort to bring new dialogical relationships into being. I've been preaching dialogue sermons for a long time. We are finding out now what some of us have known for a long time—that our stained glass, marble-floored churches are too prim and proper. Our religion has become so cold that something has to be done to defrost some of these refrigerators we call churches. The church has come dangerously close to losing the soul in religion. If your religion ain't got no soul you ought to get rid of it. The book says, "Bless the Lord, O my soul, and all that is within me, bless his holy name." (Psalm 103:1) Everybody wants to be free. And yet it is still true that we are not free. And I still long to find out why a caged bird sings?

Let me suggest to you that if I were a bird I'd want to let you know that you can cage my body but not my spirit. The poet wrote, "Stone walls do not a prison make nor iron bars a cage." You can lock me up, you can degrade me, but as long as my soul is lifted up and my spirit is on high you can't keep me caged. I've found out that nobody can ride my back as long as I stand up. My spirit hasn't learned to bow down. My spirit makes life worth living.

If I were a bird, I'd know that as long as I'm not free, the cage keeper is not free. You can't keep me down unless you stay down with me. You can't throw mud without getting dirty. I may be in a cage, but God bless your soul, you're so busy trying to keep me in the cage you might as well be in there too. This society had better learn and learn well that as long as I'm not free this society is not free. As long as one of my black, brown, red, and yellow brothers and sisters are judged by their color and not by their character we're all in a cage. The record says that while I may be in a cage you've got somebody else in that cage too. "Inasmuch as ye have done it unto the least of these my little ones you've done it unto me." (Matthew 25:40)

If I were a bird, I'd remember that this cage is not my home. The preacher of Ecclesiastes said that one day man would go to his long home. I just believe that the bars of this earthly cage will one day begin to rust and begin to rot. But "though the earthly tent of this tabernacle be destroyed, I have a building not made with hands, eternal in the heavens!" (2 Corinthians 5:1)

If I were a bird, I'd remember that one day the Liberator will come. He will come to proclaim "Good News to the poor, release to the captives, recovering of sight to the blind and to set at liberty those who are oppressed..." (Isaiah 61:1) And I believe He's coming back again!

The other day I watched a bird in his cage and after a while he began to sing. He sang on the high perch. He sang on the low perch. He sang at his bowl and he sang songs from hanging bars. Then it dawned on me that I didn't know what he was singing. And it could be he was singing:

I'm so glad trouble don't last always.

We'll understand it better by and by.

or

Soon one morning when this life is o'er,
I'll fly away.
To that home on the celestial shore
I'll fly away.

Just a few more weary days and then
I'll fly away.
To that land where joy shall never end,
I'll fly away.[4]

Ultimately, the caged bird sings because it's a terrible thing not to have a song.
Without a song the burden will be too much to bear.
Without a song the hills will be too hard to climb
Without a song the valleys will be too deep.
Without a song the rivers will be too wide.
I declare you ought to sing.

---

[4] Traditional Hymn

Every once in a while I love to sing:

Amazing grace, how sweet the sound...
I heard the voice of Jesus say...
On Jordan's stormy banks I stand...[5]

It makes no sense to sing in the face of Injustice. It makes no sense to sing in the face of racism, poverty, war, disease and hunger. But one day I met Christ for myself. And Christ has set me free. I'm foolish enough to believe that *If the Son makes you free you are free indeed!*

It makes no sense to sing but somebody said:

Why should I feel discouraged
Why should the shadows come
Why should my heart be lonely, and
Long for Heaven and Home.
When Jesus is my portion
My constant friend is He,
For His eye is on the sparrow
And I know He watches me.

I sing because I'm happy
I sing because I'm free
For His eye is on the sparrow
And I know He watches me![6]

---

[5] John Newton, "Amazing Grace," Baptist Standard Hymnal.
[6] Mrs. C.D. Martin, His Eye is on The Sparrow, *Gospel Pearls,* Nashville, TN: Sunday School Publishing Board, 1921. p. 47.

CHAPTER THREE

The Crisis of Insufficiency

❧

Metropolitan Baptist Church
1992

*A*nd as she was going to fetch it, he called to her, and said, Bring me, I pray thee, a morsel of bread in thine hand. And she said, As the Lord thy God liveth, I have not a cake but an handful of meal in a barrel, and a little oil in a cruse: and behold, I am gathering two sticks, that I may go in and dress it for me and my son, that we may eat it, and die. (1 Kings 17: 11, 12)

I believe it was the theologian Karl Barth who suggested some years ago that every preacher worthy of the name ought ascend the stairs of the pulpit with the Bible in one hand and the newspaper in the other. There is, without question, merit in that notion.

- One whose mind is absorbed only with the Bible and knows nothing of the newspaper has his soul fixed for heaven but his head is no earthly good.
- On the other hand, one whose head knows only the newspaper and nothing of the Bible, may well know what is going on in this world but will certainly be unprepared to traffic in the next.

In my reading of both, I have discovered that there is nothing that occurs in the newspaper which cannot be found in the Bible, and, conversely, the Bible comes alive when I see its truths and its testimonies walk up and down the pages of human print. That is why I am convinced that redemptive religion is terrestrial and celestial, redemptive religion is as secular as it is sacred, and ultimately deals in the realm of the human and the realm of the divine.

I share today this dictum about coming to the pulpit with the Bible in one hand and the newspaper in the other because I am disturbed that God doesn't get much time in the newspapers that I read. You can read what the President has to say, you can read of congressmen and senators, you can read of the mayor and the city council but there is not much written about what God is doing in the world. We know what Yeltsin is doing in Russia, and we know what DeKlerk is doing in South Africa, and we know what Clinton is doing in Washington but the AP and the UPI don't spend much time telling us what God's been doing lately.

And that's why today I brought the newspaper. Strange as it may seem, I found in this newspaper something of what God is doing in the world. Perhaps you did not read it because it was not to be found in the *Washington Post*. No doubt you missed the article because it was not printed in the *Dispatch* or the *Call & Post*. I found an article on what God is doing in the *Wall Street Journal* on February 26, 1992. There, on the front page no less, is a story about Annie and Walter Morgan of Marianna, Florida.

You do not know the Morgan family and neither do I, but the *Wall Street Journal* reports that this black couple—married 46 years—lived all those years in a 2-bedroom house in the segregated South, with their 18 children, in serious poverty. The *Journal* reports that they survived not because of financial means, but because of spiritual means. To read this story of Annie and Walter Morgan one could not escape the fact that here are people who know what suffering and poverty is all about. They raised their family deep in the pine woods of Florida, in a house on a red-dirt road six miles from the Alabama state line. Their only work was to till the land. And I don't care what you say, 18 mouths is a lot of mouths to feed. With six girls and twelve boys that's a lot of clothes to wash and hang on the line. With all of those children, it must have been something trying to keep life and limb together around Christmas time. And I am convinced, because the *Journal* does not tell the whole story, I am convinced that year in and year out, no doubt, the Morgan family knew what it was to live with what I have come to call The Crisis of Insufficiency.

The crisis of insufficiency of which I speak came to mind when I looked again at the Elijah narratives, found primarily in the First Book of Kings. About Elijah, the scripture says only that he was "Elijah the Tishbite, who was of the inhabitants of Gilead." (17:1) I cannot say more about him because history does not record more about him. We do not know the place of his birth or the names of his parents. We know nothing of his lineage, his history or his progeny. All we can say is that we meet him on Mt. Carmel, in the wilderness, as he confronts the 450 prophets of Baal pledged to the service of Ahab and Jezebel. And we know that his mantle fell on Elisha. But beyond this there is precious little that we can say about Elijah the Tishbite.

But we get a closer look at the life of Elijah, in the seventeenth chapter of the first book of Kings. There is recorded an encounter between Elijah and God that was pivotal in his life and is instructive for our own. You do recall, of course, that God sent Elijah with a message for Ahab: "...As the Lord God of Israel liveth, before whom I stand, there shall not be dew nor rain these years, but according to my word." (v. 1)

Whereupon God was true to His word. The heavens closed. The clouds abandoned the sky. The waters of the rivers dried up. The flow of streams and rivulets slowed to a trickle. And there stood Elijah, by the brook Cherith, waiting on the ravens to bring bread and meat both morning and evening. And soon even Elijah's brook dried up, because, as the record says, "...there had been no rain in the land." (v. 7) And I might as well pause here to tell you that, sooner or later, everybody has a Dry Brook Situation.

Whenever what you were counting on runs out, that's a dry brook situation. Whenever what used to be the sign of your strength becomes the symbol of your weakness, that's a dry brook situation. Whenever what used to be the source of your joy becomes the source of your sorrow, that's a dry brook situation. Whenever what was holding you together is gone, and you discover yourself falling apart, that's a dry brook situation. Whenever depression or loneliness or anxiety or frustration or sadness come over you and even overwhelm you, that's a dry brook situation.

And yet, in the midst of his dry brook situation, God had a remedy for Elijah:

Arise, get thee to Zarephath, which belongeth to Zidon, and dwell there: behold I have commanded a widow woman there to sustain thee. (v. 9)

It was not long, however, before Elijah realized that it looked like God had sent him from one dry brook to another. Understand

Elijah's predicament. The brooks have dried up. Even the ravens have run out of food. And God sends him to Zarephath where, according to His word, room service had already been provided. But when he got there he found "a widow woman...there gathering sticks." (v. 10) Things didn't look promising. It did not appear that provisions were available to accommodate his need. But Elijah trusted God. Elijah was willing to give God the benefit of the doubt. Elijah still believed that God was in the blessing business. And that's why, even though things looked mighty bleak, Elijah said: "Fetch me, I pray thee, a little water in a vessel, that I may drink." (v. 10)

Maybe Elijah didn't understand. The brooks have dried up. The river beds have lost their flowing streams. The water supply is gone. And Elijah says, "fetch me...a little water"! (v. 10)

But that's not all. The record says that "as she was going to fetch it, [Elijah] called to her, and said, Bring me, I pray thee, a morsel of bread in thine hand." (v. 11) Evidently, Elijah really did not understand. The brooks have dried up. There is no water for crops. The fields are parched and dry. Where there is no water there can be no wheat. Where there is no wheat there can be no meal. Where there is no meal there can be no bread.

It was in that moment that the widow of Zarephath spoke directly to Elijah. Said the widow:

> As the Lord thy God liveth, I have not a cake, but an handful of meal in a barrel, and a little oil in a cruse: and behold, I am gathering two sticks that I may go in and dress it for me and my son, that we may eat it, and die. (v. 12)

That's the story of the widow of Zarephath: I have no water, I have no meal, a little bit of oil, two sticks to make fire and after this is gone my son and I will die.

It's not that I don't want to give it to you; I just don't have it.

It's not that I'm stingy and inhospitable; I can't give what I don't have.

It's not that I'm not willing to share; the truth is there is nothing to share.

Yes, I have a little but my little is not enough.

Yes, I have a little but my little won't go very far.

Yes, I have something but it won't go very far.

And no matter what else you may say about the widow of Zarephath the reality is that she was faced with what I have come to call The Crisis of Insufficiency.

I say one ought always come to the pulpit with the newspaper in one hand and the Bible in the other because ours is a day not far removed from the circumstances of the Widow of Zarephath. I make bold to suggest today that somebody here knows what it is to live with the crisis of insufficiency.

When what you have is not enough to make ends meet that's insufficiency.

When you have a desire to give, and a cause worth giving to but it just so happens that you're fresh out of cash, that's insufficiency.

I read this newspaper and it says here that thousands, even hundreds of thousands woke up this morning without a job and that means that when they stand in line at the grocery store they will come face to face with insufficiency.

Last night in the nation's capital men and women curled up on cold cement in order to sleep through the night. But the thing that put them there in the first place, and the thing that will bring them back tonight is that somewhere they encountered insufficiency.

I keep on telling you I read this newspaper and it says that industrial plants are closing all over the country. Everyday somebody that used to be high is brought low; somebody that used to be well off is filing for bankruptcy, and somebody that used to "have it made" is having a hard time "making it." The newspaper tells us every day that the nation is reeling and rocking because of a recession that the Congress cannot handle and that the President doesn't understand. Presidential candidates are out offering answers to a problem they cannot solve; while the unemployed give up on both Democrats and Republicans, because they have come face to face with the crisis of insufficiency.

I might as well tell the truth that even church folk, those who claim they know the Lord; those who are in the church every Sunday; those who count themselves among the twice-born, blood-bought, water-washed, sons and daughters of God; even church folk don't have everything they look like they have. You better learn to look a little deeper than the surface. A whole lot of Louis Vuitton bags have no money in them. There's something strange about coming to church dressed up to beat the band when the roof is leaking, the refrigerator's empty, the back door creaks, and you're driving on "may pop" tires. All I'm trying to tell you is that there are a whole lot of folk with degrees and no job; they're educated and sophisticated but that just means they're passing out resumes all over town; they're in with the "in-crowd", they're invited to "happy hour", they're on everybody's invitation list all over town, but what you don't know is the cupboard is getting empty, and the children don't have any shoes. They're all dressed up but the rent is three months past due, no lights in the house, the gas is cut off, the phone is disconnected and when they get in the kitchen they have to "make do" on leftovers.

But I'm not making fun of anybody. Everybody in here knows what it is not to have what you need when you need it.

Everybody in here knows what it is to go to sleep at night worried about how you're going to pay bills in the morning.

Everybody in here knows what it is not to want to go to the mailbox and what it is not to want to answer the phone because the bill collector is on the other end.

Everybody in here understands what poverty is.

And if you don't know what poverty is I feel sorry for you because poverty is on the way. And whenever you come face to face with poverty you are then face to face with the crisis of insufficiency.

And so, I wanted to examine the conditions and the circumstances of the Widow of Zarephath in order to understand what it was that caused her to deal with this matter of insufficiency. Quite obviously, here was a woman who had Insufficient Means. Here was a woman who had been missed by the Poverty Program. Here was a woman who did not have the benefit of Meals on Wheels, and even though she was a widow and her son a lawful dependent there was no Aid to Dependent Children in place. Insufficiency. Here was a woman who had no Rescue Mission, or Salvation Army, or Martha's Kitchen nearby to attend to her needs. Here was a woman who even had no church to which she could turn in the time of her greatest need. All she had was a little meal, a little oil, and two sticks to rub together to make a fire. She understood the Crisis of Insufficiency.

But that wasn't her only problem. The Widow of Zarephath not only had insufficient means, she also had Insufficient Vision. You see, while it is true that her means were meager, what strikes me here is that all she saw was what she didn't have. Now, the King James Version says that Elijah asked her for "a morsel of bread," but her response was "I have not a cake." Elijah did not ask for cake, but all she could see was what she didn't have. But God does not want what we Don't Have, He wants what we Do Have! God does not want our negativity. God does not want our pessimism. God does not want a report of our poverty. The question is, "Is what you have available?" God knows when you're Out of Stock but God wants to know if He can have what you've got In Stock. Hear me today! Elijah could see what she Didn't Have, but her vision was so distorted that she was unable to see what she Did Have.

I don't mind telling you that when I grew up we didn't always have the finest cuts of meat. And sometimes the meat on the bone was mighty thin. But Mama knew how to cut the meat from around the bone and cut up a few potatoes and make gravy to put the meat and the potatoes in and before you knew it we had hash fit for a king. Mama never told us what we didn't have, she only took time to fix what we had. We thought we were eating "high on the hog."

Our slave ancestors fixed turnips for the big house, took the leaves that were left over and made turnip greens. Even slaves could tell you that no matter what you didn't have you could still keep life together with what you did have.

Well, the Widow of Zarephath had Insufficient Means, and Insufficient Vision, but ultimately she had Insufficient Faith! All Elijah asked for was a morsel of bread but she went on to discuss the limitations of her kitchen cabinet. But the reality is that her greatest insufficiency was not her Food but her Faith.

When you are in a situation of insufficiency, that's not the time to discuss economic philosophy.

When your stove has gone cold because you have nothing to cook, you really don't want to read an editorial about the economic trends that were precipitated by an agricultural downturn.

When your refrigerator is empty, you really don't want to hear a discussion on "Supply-side economics." You don't need a Ph.D. to know that what it means is that everybody else has the supply and all you've got is the demand. But I keep on telling you that the question here is not Food but Faith. You see, faith takes a holiday when you're looking at all you've got. Faith takes a back seat when your wallet is empty. Faith is hard to come by when there's only a step between you and death. Faith is nothing but religious rhetoric when buzzards have gathered overhead waiting on you to die. Faith won't hold you up when you think everything else has let you down.

Most of us have faith when the sun is shining. Faith is easy when victory is assured. Faith is easy when you've got the world in a jug and the stopper in your hand. Faith is easy when all your friends are on your side. Faith is easy when your pocketbook is full and you've got four figures in your bank account. Elijah said to the widow, "Bring me a morsel of bread." But she stopped to discuss the matter because the issue was her Faith and not her Food. All I'm trying to tell you is that the Crisis of Insufficiency will occasion an insufficient faith.

Well now, my brothers and my sisters, if you think the story of the Widow of Zarephath is only about the insufficiency of her means, her vision or her faith, then you have misunderstood the whole story. I brought you on this rather circuitous journey because Elijah's encounter with this nameless widow of Zarephath is the author's way of showing us HOW GOD WORKS despite the Crisis of Insufficiency. So, while I hold this newspaper in one hand and the Bible in the other, I want to talk about how God works with the widow, how God works with you, and how God works with the Crisis of Insufficiency.

Now then, if I read this scripture correctly, this is what it says:

And the word of the Lord came unto him, saying, Arise, get thee to Zarephath...and dwell there: behold, I have commanded a widow woman there to sustain thee. (v. 8,9)

The first thing to note in response to the Crisis of Insufficiency is that GOD SENT SOMEBODY!

You must realize that the widow was there by herself. Nobody knew she was there. Nobody else was concerned about her, or her son, or her poverty, or her meal-less, oil-less condition. But God sent somebody. Have you ever been in a situation when you didn't know what the end would be, when your telephone had stopped ringing, your friends were nowhere to be found, and you were down to your last dime. But just about that time the doorbell rang, and you said it yourself, "Child, the Lord sent you by here!" GOD SENT SOMEBODY!

There you were, in the hospital, flat on your back, unable to sit up or get up, or do for yourself but GOD SENT SOMEBODY.

There you were, in your house. Nobody there but you. Nothing to keep you company but your heartbreak. Your only companion was the blues and the only thing you felt were your tears. But just when you least expect it there's a knock on the door. GOD SENT SOMEBODY.

In your life has God ever sent somebody?

A friend to stand by your side. GOD SENT SOMEBODY.

A friend who makes a loan when your credit is bad. GOD SENT SOMEBODY.

A doctor to ease your burden. GOD SENT SOMEBODY.

A lawyer to plead your case. GOD SENT SOMEBODY.

An advocate to speak up for you. GOD SENT SOMEBODY.

A next door neighbor with a pot of soup. GOD SENT SOME-BODY.

A companion to share your lonely hours. GOD SENT SOME-BODY.

A deacon to pray for you when you couldn't pray for yourself. GOD SENT SOMEBODY.

An angel to watch over you when you couldn't watch out for yourself. GOD SENT SOMEBODY.

Ain't that just like God?

He knows when to step in on time. He sends somebody. He steps in in *Kairos* and not in *Chronos.* He sends somebody. He steps in in His time and not in our time. He sends somebody. He knows what we need before we know we need it. And then He sends some-body. He knows the answer before we ask the question. And then He sends somebody. He hears our prayers before we pray. And then He sends somebody. He makes intercessions when we can-not speak. He sends somebody. In the midst of the Crisis of Insufficiency, GOD ALWAYS SENDS SOMEBODY!

Well, the second thing that God does in response to the Crisis of Insufficiency is that HE KEEPS HIS PROMISES!

Now, this is what the scripture says:

The barrel of meal shall not waste, neither shall the cruse of oil fail until the day that the Lord sendeth rain upon the earth....And she, and he, and her house, did eat many days! (v. 14,15)

Do not lose sight of the fact that the first thing that the widow of Zarephath did was to give sacrificially of the little that she did have. And just as soon as she did God kept His promise. She kept on going to the barrel for meal, and meal kept on coming out of the barrel for her. She kept on going to the cruse for oil and oil kept on pouring out of the cruse for her.

God will keep His promise. I didn't learn this from the newspaper, I learned it from the Bible. He will keep His promise. "Give and it shall be given unto you; good measure, pressed down, and shaken together, and running over."

He will keep His promise.

If you bring your tithes and offering to the store house, He will open the windows of heaven and pour you out a blessing that there shall not be room enough to receive it. (Malachi 3:10)

He will keep His promise.

If you honor the Lord with thy substance, and with the first fruits of all thine increase: so shall thy barns be filled with plenty, and thy presses shall burst out with new wine. (Proverbs 3:9)

He will keep His promise. He which soweth sparingly shall reap also sparingly; and he which soweth bountifully shall reap also bountifully. (2 Corinthians 9:6)

He will keep His promise. "Give not grudgingly, or of necessity: for God loveth a cheerful giver." (2 Corinthians 9:7)

He will keep His promise. "Ask and it shall be given, seek and ye shall find, knock and it shall be opened unto you." (Matthew 7:7)

He will keep His promise. "My God shall supply all your need according to His riches in glory by Christ Jesus." (Philippians 4:19)

He will keep His promise. "If you trust and never doubt, He will surely bring you out, take your burden to the Lord and leave it there!"

He will keep His promise.

You can't beat God giving.
No matter how you try.
The more you give, the more He gives to you.
Just keep on giving, because it's really true.

You can't beat God giving,
No matter how you try![7]

Well, I must come to my end here. But when I came to this pulpit I brought my newspaper and I brought my Bible. And the question I have is how in the world did Annie and Walter Morgan of Marianna, Florida wind up on the front page of the most prestigious financial newspaper in the world? With all of the financial intricacies which the world is facing, who wants to know about Annie and Walter's finances? No doubt, Annie and Walter don't know anything about the stock market report that's two columns over on the same page. They don't know anything about the Dow Jones Industrial Index. They don't own any transportation stocks. They have not invested in utilities, or commodities or futures. They don't have any bonds and they don't have any T-Bills and they don't have any Zero Coupon Bonds. They don't have an investment portfolio and they don't have a personal financial advisor or individual tax analysts. But here they are—Annie and Walter on the front page of the *Wall Street Journal*. I just wonder why as I'm reading my Bible and reading my newspaper Annie and Walter Morgan wound up on the front page of the *Wall Street Journal*.

Well, I'll tell you why. The reason they wound up on the front page of the *Wall Street Journal* is that even the *Wall Street Journal* knows that they don't have the answer to the mess we're in. They've got the newspaper, and the calculators, and the financial analysts but they don't have the answer to the economic recession and the economic depression we're in. Even those who are supposed to know don't know. Bill Clinton doesn't know. Ross Perot doesn't know. And God knows George Bush doesn't know. But the *Wall Street Journal* knows that Walter and Annie know something that the smart boys just don't know.

Well, let's look at their record.

They had 18 children.

All 18 of the children graduated from high school.

Ten went on to college.

They all have good jobs.

Two brick masons, one carpenter, one chef, two in the armed

---

[7] Traditional Hymn

forces, a postal clerk, a computer operator, a teacher, a corrections officer, and three preachers.

They have 46 grandchildren and the eldest four are now in college.

Mrs. Morgan went back to school and graduated from Junior College.

Walter still farms 40 acres of their farm every day.

They taught their children how to work.

They didn't have money to buy food so they raised it.

They had no running water or electricity or heat until the 1960's.

They had no televison until the 1970's.

The children didn't have a lot of toys but they always had fun.

Their house burned down in 1957 and they lived for two years in a two room house with eleven children.

They didn't know they were poor because they had love and they had each other.

And when they asked the Morgan's, How did you make it?, when they asked the Morgan's, How did you keep your family together?, when they asked the Morgan's, How did you make it through tough economic times? Mrs. Morgan said, "Well, the Lord blessed me!"

Well, I know you've got some insufficiency in your life but if you ask your mother how she made it, she'll tell you, "The Lord blessed me." I know you don't have all you think you need but if you ask your father how he made it, he'll tell you, "The Lord blessed me." And that's all I came to tell you today, that if you trust Him, the Lord will bless you.

He will provide water when the brook has dried up—the Lord will bless you. He will provide meal when the wheat doesn't grow—the Lord will bless you. He will provide oil when it appears to have run out—the Lord will bless you.

He will send somebody when nobody else wants to be bothered—the Lord will bless you.

Has anybody here been blessed?

He will put your name on the front page of the *Wall Street Journal* even if you are from Marianna, Florida, or Waycross, Georgia, or Tougaloo, Mississippi, or Anderson, South Carolina, or Rocky Mount, North Carolina, or Baton Rouge, Louisiana. The Lord will bless you.

Somebody here had a mother and a father who could hardly make ends meet, but the Lord blessed them.

Somebody here had a mother who washed clothes in a tin tub, but the Lord blessed her.

Somebody here had a father who worked from sun up to sun down, but the Lord blessed him.

Somebody here had a mother and a father who lived in a little house, with wood floors, and a tin roof, but they loved you, and the Lord blessed them.

Somebody here had a grandfather or a grandmother who couldn't read their name, but the Lord blessed them.

Somebody here had an aunt or an uncle who gave you money for college when you didn't have any, but the Lord blessed them.

When you see how far the Lord has brought you, don't you know the Lord will bless you?

He will make a way out of no way—the Lord will bless you.

He will open doors for you—the Lord will bless you.

He will raise up friends for you—the Lord will bless you.

He will be your walking cane and your leaning post—the Lord will bless you.

He will be with you in the valley and the shadow of death—the Lord will bless you.

He will prepare a table before you in the presence of your enemies—the Lord will bless you.

He will feed you when you're hungry—the Lord will bless you.

He will give you water when you're thirsty—the Lord will bless you!

❧ II ❧
Public Prayer

CHAPTER FOUR

TransAfrica
Forum Dinner

৩৯৯৯

Prayer of Invocation
1996

OThou who is Eternal, we give Thee praise for the splendor of the moment in which we gather. We offer tonight our prayers of thanksgiving for the common things of life, for birds that sing, for flowers that bloom, for trees that bring us shade from summer's heat, for water, for grain, for flour and meal—for all the wondrous works of Your creation which sustain us.

We come in this grand hour in praise of our history, in praise of our heritage, in praise of our hope. We have come to this moment of celebration and joy—some through the water, some through the flood, some through great trials but all through the Blood.

We come in praise of our homeland, of mother Africa, whose children yet gather here tonight.

We come in praise of the cultures which bear the common thread of blood and blackness and make us rich indeed.

We come in praise of the lands that birthed us, the lands that received us, and the lands which yet nurture our people and our progeny.

We come in praise of mothers and fathers who never knew what we share here tonight.

We come in praise of Moors who brought Europe out of the Dark Ages and ushered in the Renaissance.

We come in praise of Imhotep who laid the foundation for medicine, pyramid building, military strategy, philosophy and poetry.

We come in praise of ancestors who tilled fields they did not own, cooked food they could not eat, and cleaned houses in which they could not reside.

We come in praise of a people, in Africa, in the Caribbean, in the Americas—Your children all over the world who survived in spite of the iniquities of history, Your children who thrived in spite of the atrocities of humanity, Your children who are alive in spite of systemic evil and spiritual wickedness in high places. And we come in praise of the indisputable truth that the blood which unites us is stronger than the water which divides us.

So make us mindful of our history, make us grateful for our present, make us visionary with Your hope. Bless now our coming and our sharing together, the food we eat, the wine we drink, the laughter that fills our air. In the precious Name of Jesus Christ we pray. Amen.

CHAPTER FIVE

Invocation at Public Memorial

⚜

*For Secretary of Commerce Ronald Brown
and those who accompanied him
May 1996*

Thou who art the source of light and life, we come into Your presence in this hour of tragedy and loss. We come today, in the words of our ancestors, "knee bent and body bowed, with our heads bowed beneath our knees." We come in what can only be described as "a dark midnight of the soul." We come with tears more rapid than any flowing stream. We come today with more questions than we have answers.

Yet, through our sorrow we have come with a song of thanksgiving and hope. Thanksgiving for the life of Ron Brown and for those who traveled with him. Thanksgiving for the life of one gifted by intellect and grace. Thanksgiving for his life, marked by such astounding achievement but which never lost the "common touch." Thanksgiving for this one who understood politics but never forgot people; for one who understood economics but never forgot the Harlem from which he came. Thanksgiving for one who believed that this world could be a better place in which to live, where the mind would be the measure of a man and where all would be judged by the content of their character rather than by the color of their skin.

Through our sorrow we have come with a song of thanksgiving for all those who made the journey with Ron. Those who, like him, gave their all in pursuit of a better life for all mankind. Those who, like him, gave unselfishly and tirelessly so that even those who yet reel from the ravages of war might come to know a sense of peace, and prosperity, and hope.

Through our sorrow we come to lift the family of Ron Brown and all of the families, their children, their friends, and their co-workers who know such unexplainable anguish, such indescribable pain. Give to them and to Americans the world over, in this season of distress and grief, an abiding sense of Your presence and Your power. Keep them in the center of Your perfect will so that they will not walk alone, or in despondency or despair. Teach them, and us, to walk through this storm with our heads held high, unafraid of the dark. Teach us to know that at the end of this storm is a golden strand. Give us courage to walk on through the wind, walk on through the rain, though our dreams be tossed and blown. To walk on, walk on with hope in our hearts, knowing that we'll never walk alone.

Through our sorrow in this season we come knowing that crucifixion is always followed by resurrection. We come knowing that funeral is always followed by festival. We come knowing that Good Friday is but the harbinger of Easter Sunday. We come knowing that there is a source of resurrection and life. We come knowing that death is but transition, a moment to wrap the drapery of our couch about us to lie down to pleasant dreams. We come knowing that even though the earthly tent of this tabernacle is destroyed we have another building, a house not made with hands, eternal in the heavens. We come knowing, with Job, "though He slay me, yet will I trust Him." (Job 13:15) We come knowing that when "taps" is heard on this side, "reveille" is heard on the other side. We come knowing that weeping endures for a night but joy comes in the morning. We come knowing that "...even the youths shall faint and be weary, and the young men shall utterly fall. But they that wait upon the Lord shall renew their strength. They shall mount up with wings as eagles, they shall run and not grow weary, they shall walk and not faint." (Isaiah 40:30-31)

So now, keep us. Surround us. Shield us. Until, at last, we shall meet in another world, in another sphere, in a better place. In the name of the One whom we know to be Eternal. Amen.

CHAPTER SIX

Washington Urban League

ஃ

Prayer of Invocation
Annual Banquet 1996

O Thou who art Eternal, we give Thee thanks for the blessings of this day and for the joy of this hour. Bless, we pray Thee, our coming together for the purpose of telling our story.

We have a story to tell. It is a story etched on the canvas of years gone by.

We have a story to tell, a story chiseled in the furrowed brows of our ancestors who knew the pain of labor stretched between morning's early light and the sweet sunset of summer heat.

We have a story to tell, a story stained with the blood of those ancestors hunted down by vicious dogs and hung on lynching trees.

We have a story to tell, a story of the spilled seed of children yet unborn, of babies having babies, of men locked up during the most productive years of their lives.

We have a story to tell, a story of reactionary politics, of a nation bent on shutting down the government and shutting off human services and shutting off the right of her citizens to vote.

We have a story to tell, a story of a people trapped between Republicans with a fixation on balancing the budget and Democrats running scared, afraid of losing the White House.

We have a story to tell, a story of books with pages torn out, of wooden stairs with tacks, and of always being last hired and first fired.

But thanks be to God we have another story to tell. We have a story to tell of achievement despite the odds, of victory snatched from defeat, of accomplishment scholars said could never take place.

We have a story to tell, a story of a people oppressed who have learned how to run through troops, leap over walls, squeeze through rocks, step over stones, walk through barriers and push through obstacles.

Thank God we have another story to tell.

We can tell the story of how we made it over.

We can tell the story of how our souls have been anchored.

We can tell the story of how crucifixion is always followed by resurrection.

We can tell the story that weeping may endure for a night but joy comes in the morning.

We thank You that we can say tonight, "This is my story, this is my song, praising my Savior all the day long."

Thank You for this hour.

Thank You for this moment.

Thank You for the Washington Urban League, for its leaders, those who work tirelessly among and for our people. Thank You for this celebration of social achievement and victory.

Thank You for the stories that we yet will tell of Your goodness, Your mercy and Your grace.

Bless our coming together, our food, our friends, our fellowship. And, at last bind us to each other as we are bound together with Thee. In the Name of Him Whom to know is life and life everlasting.

Amen.

CHAPTER SEVEN

A Eulogy

༄

For David A. Clarke, Chairman
District of Columbia City Council
April 4, 1997

*B*ut go thou thy way till the end be: for thou shalt rest, and stand
in thy lot at the end of the days.
*But you, go your way, and rest; you shall rise for your reward at the
end of the days.* [NRSV] (Daniel 12:13)

I rise to speak today because David was not just a part of this
community, Dave was part and parcel of this community. I rise to
speak today because, even though it may be politically incorrect to
say so, I believe Dave loved the Lord, I believe Dave was convert-
ed, I believe Dave was saved. And if I knew Dave at all, Dave
would not want a sad funeral. Dave would not want a sad eulogy.
I suspect that David would authorize me to tell it just like it is.

The book of Daniel, much like the book of Revelation, is a writing borne on the wings of the mysterious and the enigmatic. Not
only so, this is a writing which uses ancient and cryptic language
to reveal divine truths which are as fresh as sunrise and as modern as morning.

I do not know why Dave Clarke was drawn to this book as often
as he quite obviously was. There was, I suspect, something of a
preacher down in Dave's soul and every chance he got he always
made his way swiftly to this book known as Daniel. I never heard
him quote the words of Isaiah's comfort and hope. I never heard
him speak the dark words of Jeremiah's spiritual depression and
inescapable judgment. Nor did I ever hear him tell of Ezekiel's
vision or his visit to that valley of sun-bleached and dry bones. But
he did speak of this strange and often misunderstood writing. He
did speak of this work which scholars call apocalyptic. He did
speak of this work which some have suggested even its author did
not understand. He did speak of this work which contains a vision

of the future and describes the course of world history, through the use of symbols which mere mortals are hard pressed to understand. I do not know why he did, but he did speak of this man named Daniel.

I shall not labor long with this writing, one familiar even to the most modest Bible student among us. Every Sunday School child knows of those four Hebrew boys, exiles though they were, who found themselves living under the reign of Nebuchadnezzar, King of Babylon, six centuries before Christ. Their names were Belteshazzar, Hananiah, Mishael and Azariah, or as is their more common usage, Daniel, Shadrach, Meshach, and Abednego. It is a story which speaks of Daniel in the den of lions, the three Hebrew boys in their fiery furnace, and that's the whole of it.

In the main, however, this book has more to do with a man whose life was spent somewhere between the urging of his own spiritual sensitivities and an inescapable political reality. Here was a man who worked at the behest of the kings who sat on Babylon's throne but who never forgot his allegiance to God nor his commitment to the people from whose loins he had come. To be quite honest about it, Daniel was part politician and part preacher. He had a praying side but he also had a practical side. He had a head for heaven but his feet were on the earth. He always found himself standing somewhere between God and government, always standing in that tension between earthly power and ultimate power.

I suspect, however, that Dave Clark may have been drawn to this book primarily because it deals with THE POLITICS OF GOD.

Daniel deals with a people who are caught in a suffering situation. That's politics.

Daniel deals with a people whose social situation demands that they live with less than they need and whose pain seems greater than their ability to bear it. That's politics.

Daniel deals with a political power structure that is bent on the exaltation of the throne, which knows no value but silver and gold, and where faith is secondary to the rule of law. That's politics.

This is a book which raises the issues of the politics of God. Perhaps David wanted to know about the politics of God. Is God a Republican or a Democrat?

Is God liberal, conservative, or somewhere in between?

Is God pro-choice or right-to-life?

Is God a socialist or a capitalist?

Is God more on the side of individual liberty or governmental authority?

What are the politics of God?

The homeless still make up their beds on the streets of the capital of the free world. What are the politics of God?

There is something strange here. People who are required to pay taxes but are still denied the right to vote.

A few of us on the inside are running for office, while those who live on the outside are running for their lives. What are the politics of God?

Or, to put the question yet another way:

If God is just, why then is there injustice?

If God is rich, why then are the poor yet among us?

If God is a liberator, then why are we yet imprisoned?

If God sets men free, then how free are we?

Look about us...

We are not free spiritually.

We are not free from profane materialism.

We are not free from vulgar sensuality.

We are not free from invidious racism.

We are not free from cultural arrogance and contempt for the weak and the powerless.

I know we give lip-service to the separation of church and state but all of us might as well agree that there is always religion in politics and there is certainly politics in religion. That's why I would like to know: what are the politics of God?

I believe that by the telling of Daniel's story Dave Clark discovered some lessons, timeless in their import and in their impact, that are left for you and for me.

Remember if you will, that when Daniel and the three Hebrew boys were taken into captivity they were set apart to be cultivated and nurtured at the hand of the king. This book suggests that King Nebuchadnezzar had determined to teach them with the finest instructors of his realm, to feed them with meat and the delicacies from the royal table, and to satisfy their thirst with his wine. But this book says that: "...Daniel purposed in his heart that he would not defile himself with the portion of the king's meat, nor with the wine he drank." (Daniel 1:8)

Daniel purposed in his heart. The lesson here is that in the life of every man there comes a time when a decision has to be made to stand up for what you believe. Daniel's dietary decision was not popular. Daniel's decision was not popular among his peers. It was not popular among his political advisors. But Daniel had made up his mind—he had purposed in his heart—that no matter, what he would not eat the king's meat.

No matter what one might say about David Clarke, one could always say that Dave was a man who stood for something. You may not have agreed with him; his politics might have been unpopular; you might have questioned how a white man could have such a position of importance in a majority black city. The reason for it was that he stood for something. You might not have liked him, you might not have agreed with him, but when his mind was made up his mind was made up.

The second lesson to be found in the Daniel narrative is that Daniel knew how to read God's writing. You recall, of course, that when the nation was in its most vulnerable and weakened condition Belshazzar made a great feast and drank wine before thousands. Signs of decay were all about the kingdom. The moral fiber of the nation was at its lowest ebb. Politically, socially and economically the nation was at the point of ruin. That conditions were ripe for God to move in and about the kingdom was apparent to even the most casual observer. And yet, that's the time that the king decided to throw a party. That's the time the king decided to get high. That's the time the king decided to get wasted. The eyes of the whole world were on him and that's when he decided to drink himself under the table.

And when the handwriting appeared on the wall...*MENE, MENE, TEKEL UPHARSIN*...even blind men could see that the days of the kingdom were numbered, that the king himself had been weighed in the balance and found wanting, and that the kingdom had been divided, but nobody could read the writing but Daniel.

I rise to say today that in the affairs of men and nations, every once in a while you need somebody who can read the handwriting of God. That is why [when an interpreter was needed] the queen advised Nebuchadnezzar that "There is a man in thy kingdom in whom is the spirit of God." (Daniel 5:11) If not a Daniel, if not a David Clarke, surely there must be someone in the kingdom who is acquainted with the affairs of God.

If the society is to be saved there must be someone who is on intimate terms with the Eternal. If the city is to be saved, if the nation is to be redeemed, there must be someone whose hands have not been defiled and whose steps are ordered by the Lord.

Dave Clarke ever pointed his finger toward Daniel, I believe, because he could clearly see the source of authentic power. You do remember, of course, that those three Hebrew boys were thrown into a fiery furnace, fired seven times hotter than its normal course. And yet, when they were offered the choice to bow or to burn they uttered words which have resounded through the annals of time:

> ...Our God whom we serve is able to deliver us from the burning fiery furnace, and he will deliver us out of thine hand, O king. But if not, be it known unto thee, O king, that we will not serve thy gods, nor worship the golden image which thou hast set up.
> (Daniel 3:17-18)

There is a spiritual lesson here. There was no doubt in the mind of those boys that God had authentic power. Their position was, however, that even if God failed to be God they still would not bow down. In other words God will do what God says God will do, but if not—even if God won't—we'll trust Him anyhow.

God has the power to do the impossible; but even if it becomes impossible for God to achieve the impossible we'll serve Him anyhow.

God has the power to rescue men and nations from the ravages of roaring lions or the licking flames of torrid heat but if not we'll stand with Job and say, "Though he slay me, yet will I trust him." (Job 13:15)

You know the end of this story. Shadrach, Meshach, and Abednego bound in their coats, hats and other garments, were led to the fiery furnace and cast in. But because the ovens had been heated seven times hotter than usual, the men that threw them into the furnace were themselves burned by the heat.

But that's not all. Nebuchadnezar could not sleep that night. All night long he tossed and turned. Early the next morning he went down to the fiery furnace to see for himself what had happened to those three Hebrew boys. There he stood, wiping sleep out of his eyes.

"Did not we cast three men bound into the midst of the fire?" (Daniel 3:24) And the answer returned: "Yes, King, we threw three men Shadrach, Meshach, and Abednego into the fire." But the King replied: "I see three men but I also see a fourth and he looks like the Son of God." (Daniel 3:25) [NRSV]

And that's what I came to tell you today. Dave Clarke sent me here to tell you that he did not die, God just snatched him out of the fire. Dave Clarke sent me here to tell you that he did not die, God just snatched him from the lion's jaw. Dave Clarke sent me to tell you that you can depend on God. He didn't just save the three Hebrew boys from the fire, but neither did their clothes smell like fire nor was a hair on their heads singed or burned.

You can depend on God. It is no secret what God can do. What He's done for others, He'll do for you.

You can depend on God. Through the storm, through the rain, through sickness, through pain, you can depend on God. May I tell you why you can depend on Him? If this were church on Sunday morning I'd tell you, He's able. Dave Clarke made his way into this church every Sunday morning because he knew that God is able. You can depend on Him because He's able. Able to save you. Able to secure you. Able to strengthen you. Able to keep you from falling. He's able to present you faultless before His Father. I said, He's able. If you've ever been in your own lion's den, you know He's able. In the midnight hour, He's able. In sorrow's valley, He's able. At death's door, He's able. When you're all alone, He's able. When you don't know what the future holds, He's able. As long as you know He holds the future, you know He's able.

I cannot come to the end of this homily with only a word for us who remain. I suspect that there is a word here in the closing lines of the book of Daniel which was meant solely for Dave. After all the pain and the sorrow, the heartache and the heartbreak which Daniel experienced there was at the end a word just for him. After all of Dave's suffering, after all of Dave's ups and downs, after all of Dave's political ins and outs, I believe Dave referred to this book so often because in the end there is a word here just for him. And this what it says: "But you, go your way, and rest; you shall rise for your reward at the end of the days." (Daniel 12:13) [NRSV]

Dave, go your way and rest.

Go your way and rest...lie down for an eon or two.

Go your way and rest...wrap the drapery of your couch about you and lie down to pleasant dreams.

Go your way and rest...until the wicked cease from troubling and weary souls shall be at rest.

Go your way and rest...until morning stars sing together and the sons of God shout for joy.

Go your way and rest...until every day is Sunday and Sabbaths have no end.

Go your way and rest...rocked in the bosom of Abraham.

Go your way and rest...safe in the arms of Jesus.

Go your way and rest...there'll be no need for a quorum, no need for a committee of the whole, no need for a binding resolution, no need for gavels, or rallies or fundraisers, or any of the rest.

Go your way and rest. You shall rise for your reward at the end of the days.

Good night, sweet prince. May guardian angels guide thee to thy rest!

❧ III ❧
Addresses

CHAPTER EIGHT

A Question of Profit and Loss

⚜

Remarks on the occasion of the graduation of eighteen students of color from the Kenan Flagler School of Business, The University of North Carolina, Chapel Hill, on Sunday, May 15, 1993 by the proud father of Henry Beecher Hicks, III.

We have come today to share the joy of the achievement of the Class of 1993 as they graduate from the Kenan Flagler School of Business. As the father of one of your classmates, H. Beecher Hicks, III, I have the high honor of standing in the place of your parents, grandparents, siblings, aunts and uncles, wives, loves and significant others as you mark yet another milestone in your academic careers. I know that I am not alone when I join them in saying, *To God be the glory for the things He hath done!*

It is not insignificant that on this day you have asked for me to share from a book that never appeared on your **required** or **suggested** reading lists. This is so, I suppose, because most often the world does not consider Jesus to be concerned about matters of business.

I take a different point of view, however. If you really want to learn some business principles that will be lasting and true, consult with Jesus.

- At the age of twelve He was found debating with doctors and arguing with lawyers because He was involved in what He described as *My Father's Business!*
- One afternoon, at a wedding festival in Cana of Galilee He turned six waterpots into wine and set in motion an approach to supply and demand that John Locke has yet to consider. That's business!
- This book says He fed five thousand one day with only two

fish and five loaves of bread; somehow He managed to multiply by dividing and when it was over He had more than He had
when He started out. That's production, inventory control and
management. That's business!

- He stopped by a seaside and found Peter, James and John at
their fishing trade, told them to put up their nets and follow
Him to become fishers of men. Changing one business for
another...it sounds like mergers and acquisitions to me. That's
business!

- It was on a Sabbath morn that Jesus stopped by the synagogue
and turned over the tables of the money changers. And all of
this was, as you know, before Michael Milken, before junk
bonds, before the closing of saving and loans, and even before
the Resolution Trust Corporation. His language was not sophisticated but it was precise: "It is written my house shall be called
a house of prayer but you have made it a den of thieves." (Luke
19:46) Sounds like a corporate take-over. That's business!

Beyond all of this, however, there is a word about business
embedded in Matthew's recording of the words of Jesus:

> For whosoever will save his life shall lose it: and whosoever will
> lose his life shall find it. For what is a man [or woman] profited if
> he shall gain the whole world and lose his soul? (Matthew 16:26)

Jesus Himself raises the critical question of losing and finding, of
profit and loss. Or, stated in the reverse, in business it is possible
to gain but it is also possible to lose.

Briefly, at this pinnacle of your achievement, there are some
things you newly minted MBA's ought never lose:

NEVER LOSE YOUR RELATIONSHIP WITH EACH OTHER. You
eighteen students whom this country calls minorities but who represent the majority of the people of the world, never forsake each
other. It is not by accident that you are called to this place at this
moment. Over these two years you have forged a network of caring and support. You are now, in the words of Martin King, "inex-
tricably interwoven and intertwined into a garment of mutuality."
Yours is a common destiny. Maintain your relationships. Nurture
your friendships. Become together what you can never become
alone. Invest in each other and, in so doing, strengthen the whole.

As you gain the world today, be careful that tomorrow you do not lose your soul. It's really just a question of profit and loss.

NEVER LOSE YOUR RELATIONSHIP WITH YOUR HERITAGE. You represent the highest and the best, the off-spring of those who came across the seas to slavery and the auction blocks of our painful history. Tomorrow you will put your feet on the cold marble of corporate America. You will sit in boardrooms and make decisions among the highest echelons of capitalism. You will live in houses your parents cannot afford, drive automobiles your grandparents could never imagine, and draw paychecks larger even than your own expectations and which most probably overstate your real worth. But you must not forget that the pay you receive is not yours alone but represents reparations long overdue to your ancestors. Your negotiated salary ought to factor in the pain and the suffering of those who are leaning over the battlements of glory cheering you on. Never forget your heritage. Never be ashamed of the birthright of your blackness. Let it be the foundation upon which you stand, never the crutch upon which you lean. Today you gain the whole world. Tomorrow do not lose your soul. It's really a question of profit and loss.

Finally, NEVER LOSE YOUR RELATIONSHIP WITH THE ONE WHO MADE THIS DAY POSSIBLE. Here you are—our best and our brightest. Here you are tall, black and proud. Whoever you are, however, whoever you become, it is not by your power but by a power greater than your own. You learned about how to get an appropriate return on your investment. Remember, however, that your spiritual dividends will accrue only as a direct result of your investment, and that spiritual truths can't be calculated. Remember the words of Solomon: "Wisdom is the principal thing; therefore get wisdom: and with all thy getting, get understanding." (Proverbs 4:7)

Just think of it:

You can now take at seat at the Stock Exchange; program our computers; analyze market indicators; and manage, merchandise and control our commodities. In a sense, you have gained the whole world.

So teach our people to be producers rather than consumers.

Marshal the rich resources that will enable us to invest in our future rather than repeat our past.

Run our businesses, start up banks, establish international liaisons, forge trade agreements, become CEO's and CFO's, join the jet set. Don't just visit Wall Street...own Wall Street! Be the best that you can be.

Still, when it is done, remember that God made it possible.

God opened this door.

God made this way.

God moved this mountain.

God held back the enemy.

God parted the waters of the Red Sea.

God held back the lion's jaw.

God took the heat out of the fire.

You didn't do it, God did it! This is your day to say: "The Lord hath done great things for us, whereof we are glad!" (Psalm 126:3)

Today you gain the whole world. Tomorrow do not lose your soul. It's a question of profit and loss.

CHAPTER NINE

Challenge to the African American Church

Problems and Perspectives for the Third Millennium

The Keynote Address delivered on the occasion of the Second Annual National Conference of The Information and Services Clearinghouse, Howard University School of Divinity, Washington, D. C., on Monday, October 17, 1994. Revised for publication.

*A*nd *Jesus came and spake unto them, saying, All power is given unto me in heaven and in earth. Go ye therefore, and teach all nations, baptizing them in the name of the Father, and of the Son and of the Holy Ghost: Teaching them to observe all things whatsoever I have commanded you: and, lo, I am with you alway, even unto the end of the world. Amen.* (Matthew 28:18-20)

There can be little question or debate that these are critical times for the African American Church. Our gathering is profound testimony of our love as well as our concern for both the organization and the organism we call the church. Further still, our gathering comes at a crisis point in the history of the modern Christian Church—rarely has the Church been under greater attack from forces within and without, rarely has the Church been so completely engaged in a spiritual warfare with "principalities and powers, against spiritual wickedness in high places." Fundamentally, however, we may agree at the outset that the African American Church is not now what it has been nor what it must become, if it is to honor its past or justify its future.

Our discussion will be secure with an acknowledgment that the African American Church, as a consequence of the legacy of suffering and oppression of its members, is distinctively different from other religious gatherings. It is also a premise of this address that the church in the African American tradition has been and continues to be primarily Christian, and that the foundation of her witness is the inexhaustive adequacy of the Word of God as revealed in Jesus Christ. This presentation, then, is made from a philosophical standpoint which is undeniably African and unapologetically Christian.

Let me establish at the outset my personal commitment to the cause of Christ and His Church. I am, in every sense of the word, a child of the parsonage and a product of the church. Precisely because of my love for and commitment to the Church I am obligated to critically examine her future, and to expose my views to the scrutiny of both the academic and professional theological community. At the invitation of the Information and Services Clearinghouse of the Howard University School of Divinity, I have been asked to write a word of challenge to the African American Church. If such a word is to have integrity, then it must be articulated with boldness and without fear. To this formidable task we now turn.

The frame and focus of my discussion is set by these words:

> There is a tendency in Churches during times of social upheaval or revolutionary change to avoid the real issue by calling the people back to God, which almost always means calling them back to the way they used to practice their religion in the churches.
>
> Until the churches today face squarely, honestly, and courageously the real issue of what their relationship should—and must—be to a society which is highly organized, secular and technological in character, and what specific and concrete forms their contact and communication with society should take, they cannot command the attention of men nor effectually perform their reconciling ministry among them.[8]

These words were written by the late Dr. Jesse Jai McNeil in *Mission in Metropolis,* fully three decades ago. It was clear then, as it is now, that the African American Church must soberly and honestly face the challenges which the future presents. There is no

---

[8] McNeil, Jesse Jai, *Mission in Metropolis,* Grand Rapids, MI: William B. Eerdmans Publishing Company, 1965, pp. 10-11.

doubt that these are "times of social upheaval or revolutionary change." Ours is certainly a society which is "highly organized, secular and technological in character." However, the nature of the change and upheaval we are experiencing far exceeds McNeil's vision. The dimensions of that change have quite possibly surpassed the assumptions of those of us pursuing legitimate and authentic ministry.

By and large, the churches which I see—most of which are African American—seem to be little more than anemic, impotent specters of the first Church at Pentecost, having neither her breath, her wind, her fire, nor her power. Change...revolutionary upheaval...is all about the Church. Our problem, it seems to me, is that we have failed to grasp either spiritually or intellectually the sociological and theological changes which the Church is destined to endure.

At the close of the twentieth century, the Church is facing forces which must be clearly understood. The theological pluralism currently in vogue in many academic settings is no more than a satanic attack against the Church.

The Church is undergoing such radical internal changes and theological shifts that within the next quarter century you and I may not be able to recognize her. If what we are seeing today is a harbinger of the Church of the twenty first century, then we may expect that all barriers of tradition will soon come down. Any vestige of religious restriction will be gone. Biblical teachings will be compromised. Denominations will be buried. The moral authority of the church will be a thing of the past. There will be no such thing as *sin.* Nothing will be sacred. Any church members who remain will believe as they will, do as they wish, and the Bible will be no more than a curious reference book on a shelf of interesting but irrelevant spiritual literature.

It would appear that the church has forgotten the power and the priorities which first brought her into existence. Instead of transforming the culture, the church has chosen to conform to the culture. Roger L. Frederikson has suggested that we have reached the point that "[w]e have been so domesticated and institutionalized within the ghetto of the religious establishment that we have been cut off and alienated from the very people we have been eager to reach." [9]

---

[9] Frederikson, Roger L., *The Communicator's Commentary,* John Lloyd J. Ogilvie, General Editor, Waco, TX: Word Books, 1987, p. 31.

Within the African American church, we seem to have at least two societies, separate and unequal. From its inception, the African American church was a place of refuge and redemption for the oppressed and the disadvantaged. The church was a haven for those who had little, and prospects for less. The church was a safe harbor for the undernourished, the ill-fed, and the ill-housed. In days gone by the church was—in the words of William Augustus Jones of the Bethany Church in Brooklyn, New York—"where beggars came to tell other beggars where to find bread."

In the last decade of the twentieth century, however, it appears that a reversal has taken place. No longer is the African American church clearly identified with the oppressed. Rather, in many instances membership in the African American Church is now one more badge of social status. Church membership is *in.* Church membership is *politically correct.* The church is high on the social agenda of many African Americans.

Far too many unite with the church for reasons which have nothing whatsoever to do with an authentic conversion, by whatever definition such an experience is known. At the close of the twentieth century, the church has been infiltrated by a strange collection of *consumer Christians* who hop from church to church until their needs are met or until something more popular comes along. Cable television and other forms of media technology have created a competitive frenzy for the membership of those who bring a *shopping mall mentality* to their pursuit for religious meaning. Perhaps that is why it is true that "much of our so called 'Christian Fellowship' has waded in the shallow [waters] of human effort and organization rather than swimming in the deep waters of God's organism and power." [10] Roger Frederikson has appropriately suggested that we are in an era of "...technological gimmicks...a religion that has become slick and manipulative and marketable." [11]

The consequence of these realities is that the African American Church—no longer revolutionary, no longer a drum major for social justice—appears to be out of step with the masses. The church seems to be no longer filled by the Higher Spirit who empowers her.

Critical questions must be asked. Who better to ask these questions than the professional teachers and practitioners of religion?

---

[10] Ibid., p. 31.
[11] Ibid., p. 31.

Cornel West has properly and appropriately pointed to what he calls "the crisis of black leadership." [12] Where is that seminal fluid within the African American Church tradition which has historically given birth to charismatic leadership and consecrated scholarship? Where are the black preachers who are not afraid to dig deep into our ancient African ancestry and stimulate a laity who fill both church and community with vigorous, radical, and spirit-filled intellectualism?

At a time when large portions of the African American community are in social, economic, and spiritual crisis, the African American Church must defend herself against charges of irrelevance. From the cloistered walls of our seminaries and the sterile walls of our sanctuaries the theologians, Biblical exegetes, apologists and preachers of the African American church are unable to make her either relevant or meaningful.

By my estimation there are at least two generations of African Americans who are so thoroughly alienated from the church that they will desecrate a church which they no longer see as sacred and dismiss preachers they no longer see as important. In a real sense, the church *drop-outs* of the sixties and seventies have produced the spiritually bankrupt and Biblically illiterate generation of the nineties. Now it appears that the sins of the fathers have indeed been visited upon the children. Quite frankly, I am convinced that if we fail to address these realities within the next half century the African American Church we love may very well be dead, embalmed in the fluid of theological irrelevance and buried in demonic ecclesiastical gamesmanship.

What then are the challenges which must be faced by the African American Church?

I. SOCIOECONOMIC CHALLENGES

The African American Church must take the lead in addressing the socioeconomic needs of its fellowship. The church cannot ignore the staggering statistics which describe too many black communities.

While the majority of black Americans are making economic gains, for a chronically poor subgroup of black America, conditions are deteriorating with no improvement in sight. These blacks reside

---

[12] West, Cornel, *Race Matters,* Boston: Beacon Press, 1993, p. 33.

primarily in ghetto neighborhoods and are the most disadvantaged persons and families, many dependent on welfare. Female-headed families are the norm and almost 80 percent of African American children born in predominantly black neighborhoods are born out of wedlock.

Seventy-eight percent of the murder victims in 1991 were males; and 89 percent were persons 18 years of age or older. Forty-eight percent were aged 20 through 34 years. An average of 50 of every 100 were black. Ninety-three percent of the black murder victims were slain by black offenders.[13]

Over the past thirty years the African American community has experienced a 1000% increase in violent crime, a 400% increase in teenage suicides and a 700% increase in households headed by single women.

The real challenge to the African American Church is this: African Americans have the fastest growing AIDS rate, the highest teenage pregnancy rate, the second highest school drop-out rate and the highest rate of drug-driven violence in the nation. It is clear that the African American church must intentionally refocus its ministries to address these social and economic dilemmas. While there are numerous examples of churches across the nation engaged in significant ministries designed to reverse these socioeconomic conditions, the sad reality is that these are exceptions, not norms.

Unfortunately, it is also true that the major denominations have failed to harness the collective African American economic power resident in the churches, or to create socially responsive ministries of national scope and significance. While our denominations boast memberships in the millions, the power those numbers represent have yet to be guided toward any agenda for massive social change. In a word, black denominational structures are not taken seriously in any quarter. Having denied the divine power source which has the capacity to bring and insure life, African American denominations apparently have no power—social, economic or spiritual. Too often, the wealth of African American denominations has been used to foster the personal economic power of church leaders rather than the collective economic power of the masses they represent and should serve.

---

[13] Congressional Black Caucus Foundation, Inc., *The Face of Black America: Looking to the 21st Century*, Washington D.C.: Congressional Black Caucus,1992.

So critical is the condition of black denominations that we are witnessing the dawn of a post-denominational era. If this trend can be reversed, and I doubt that it can, we can no longer be engaged in business as usual. The Reverend Kirbyjon Caldwell of the Windsor Village United Methodist Church in Houston, Texas sums it best:

> Churches really have two choices—they can either be monuments representing what used to be or mission stations designed to meet the current and anticipated needs of the community.[14]

The revolution must be real. The revolution must be radical. The revolution must start in the Church.

II. CULTURAL INTRUSION

Those who are serious students of the church and who are at all sensitive to shifts in public policy are aware of a movement which I call cultural intrusion into the affairs of the church. Sadly, the Church—once a citadel of faith—is now viewed as little more than a secular auditorium, its purposes to be no more respected than those of any other social agency. While at one time the church was sacrosanct, revered as a vital part of the community, the practice of institutional religion is now under attack by the Congress of the United States. Local government agencies, siding with organized community and civic groups, have blocked the church from fulfilling her ministry to "do unto the least of these." Indeed, the whole idea of the autonomy of religion, preserved in our form of government, is now subject for review.

In his book *The Culture of Disbelief*, Stephen L. Carter has made bold and arresting observations about the intrusion of the culture into the affairs of the church, particularly in relationship to the continuing effort to dissolve the church's first amendment protections. The church, of course, becomes the target of the culture whenever the church becomes prophetic and/or moves to contradict and challenge the assumptions or preferences of the culture. Carter suggests that "...our public culture more and more prefers religion as something without political significance, less an independent moral force than a quietly irrelevant moralizer, never heard, rarely seen." [15]

---

[14] Kirbyjon Caldwell, *Jesus as the New Paradigm*, The Forum Files, Tyler, TX: Leadership Network, 4(3). August 1994, p.2.
[15] Carter, Stephen L., *The Culture of Disbelief*, New York: Basic Books, 1993, p.9.

What has occurred in Washington, D. C., is mirrored in cities throughout the nation. Here attempts have been made to prevent churches from feeding the hungry, sheltering the homeless, or expanding facilities in neighborhoods whose residents prefer gentrification that maintains neighborhood exclusivity. What is afoot, however, is a direct assault on the right of the church to pursue her God-given ministry. Carter goes on to suggest that

> "...the principal purpose of the metaphorical wall of separation between church and state was always to prevent governmental interference with a religion's decisions about what its own theology requires." [16]

The issue I raise requires far more extensive discourse than is possible here. Nevertheless, let us state unequivocally that the Church must never capitulate to the culture nor forsake her sacred mission. We must be vigilant against this secular assault on the traditional mission fo the church. Even now we are experiencing a concomitant secularization of the church itself. In the words of historian Viscount Bryce:

> The more the church identified with the world, the further did it depart from its own best self. The Church expected or professed to Christianize the world, but in effect the world secularized the Church. [17]

I cannot state more forcefully that, if the church is to survive and flourish, she must resist the contamination of the culture in whatever form it appears. If there is revolution there must also be resistance. Our resistance must be real. Our resistance must be radical. Our resistance can save the Church.

III. ECCLESIASTICAL EROSION

It is clear that revolutionary and radical change is on the doorstep of the African American Church. These dramatic changes spell the creation of a new African American church whose spirit is changing, whose complexion is being altered, and whose leadership is being challenged in profound ways. So numerous are these challenges, in fact, that they can only be mentioned in passing.

---

[16] Ibid., p.39.
[17] Ibid., p.81.

First. The Death of Denominationalism.

Historically, African Americans have been deeply loyal to denominational affiliations. Drive through any town in American and you would find the Baptist Church, the Methodist Church, and down the road and off to the left, the local Holiness church. In the last decade of the twentieth century, we are witnessing not only the gradual disappearance of these ecclesiastical labels, but even slow forsaking of the word *church*. "Word" churches, "Community" churches and a variety of "fellowships" now clutter the ecclesiastical landscape. In *A Generation of Seekers*, Wade Clark Roof indicates that one third of those who grew up in mainline Protestantism have switched denominations. He suggests that the meaning of this change has to do with a reemergence of spirituality, religious and cultural pluralism and multilayered belief and practice.[18] Roof goes on to suggest that:

The changing patterns of family and religion...are crucial. High rates of interfaith marriage and continuing large numbers of blended families will result in new generations of children with weak institutional ties. Denominational boundaries within Protestantism will likely erode further, as increasing numbers of Americans grow up knowing very little about their religious heritage.[19]

In this connection, one cannot fail to mention the recent birth of the Full Gospel Baptist Fellowship, conceived in the heart of Bishop Paul S. Morton, Pastor of Greater St. Stephens in New Orleans, Louisiana. In a personal interview with this writer, Bishop Morton said that this Fellowship is not designed to threaten or replace mainline denominations, but to provide an opportunity for those who wanted to remain Baptist and yet exercise *all* of the gifts of the Spirit, particularly speaking in tongues.

The Full Gospel Baptist Fellowship has gained the attention of the African American church community primarily because of the introduction of Bishops within the Baptist Church. With the exception of Primitive Baptists and other smaller segments of the denomination, Bishops are clearly not a part of the polity of mainstream Baptists. The Baptist Church, says Morton, has failed to use the office of

[18] Roof, Wade Clark, *A Generation of Seekers,* San Francisco, CA: Harper, 1993, p.177.
[19] Ibid., p.249.

Bishop not because of any biblical prohibition but merely because of tradition. In this, of course, Morton has failed to acknowledge that Baptists have a strong congregational ecclesiology which precludes the hierarchical structure he is necessarily bringing to birth. As he has created a Council of Bishops[20] which literally spans the country, the Full Gospel Fellowship gathered over 30,000 delegates in its initial meeting last July. Most pastors who have embraced this movement are tired of do-nothing Boards and other layers of political structures within the Baptist Church, which they view as obstacles to accomplishment of the mission of the church and deterrents to the minister's sense of purpose and calling.

According to the Reverend Dr. Kevin Cosby of the St. Stephen Baptist Church of Louisville, Kentucky, Morton's success may be attributed to his ability to communicate the Christian message through a medium which is readily understood by the "baby-boomer, baby buster" culture. This ability, in fact, may be a more compelling factor in the attraction of this fellowship than speaking in tongues. This movement clearly seeks to escape the "churchiness" of the traditional, strait-laced bourgeois black church. More to the point, it is also a radical departure from mainline Baptist theology, and represents a serious new element of pentecostalism within the Baptist family. While it is technically not a denomination, its numbers are too large, its growth too rapid, and its broad base of appeal too obvious to be ignored.

The death of denominationalism is a serious factor on the African American religious scene. It would appear that we have failed to appropriate the lessons of the past in ways which would bring renewal and life to the Church. I believe, however, that the radical and revolutionary change we are experiencing may be the breath of fresh air the church has needed. Indeed, this *new thing* God is doing may be both *wind* and *fire* for the redemption of His Church.

Second. The Rise of Pentecostalism.

We must take seriously what began as the Azusa Street Revival in Los Angeles, California in 1906. What began in a stable by William Joseph Seymore has become a religious movement of unparalleled proportions. Specifically we must not forget that Pentecostalism in America began as an interracial movement with

---

[20] Typically early middle aged, these Bishops are consummate preacher/pastors who share an inability to break through the ranks of leadership in traditional denominations.

a black preacher at its helm. At the apex of Jim Crow in America, William Seymore said that the *color line [had] been washed away by the blood.* From this movement came the Church of God in Christ, (C.O.G.I.C) but also the Assemblies of God.

To tell the truth, within the African American community and particularly within the more traditional denominations, there has always been the tendency on the part of many to look down their noses at Pentecostals. Typically considered lower class blacks, they were ridiculed as *Holy Rollers,* often called fanatics, and were viewed as unstable whenever speaking in tongues was discussed. If we are to take seriously the challenges facing the African American Church, however, we must face the implications of the rise of Pentecostalism. According to Dr. Harvey Cox of the Harvard Divinity School, we would do well to consider the following:

- There are **400 million** Pentecostals in the world. It is the fastest growing Christian movement on earth, growing even faster than Islam. C.O.G.I.C. is the fastest growing denomination in the United States.
- The major growth of Pentecostalism has been in urban rather than rural areas. It appears that Pentecostalism is the religion of choice among the poor.
- The focus of Pentecostalism is not on doctrine, organization or behavior. Rather, its focus centers on religious experience, primarily the baptism of the Holy Spirit.
- There are a variety of movements, churches and denominations within Pentecostalism. There is no ecclesiastical hierarchy; there are no creeds or anything else which holds the movement together other than the movement of the Holy Spirit.
- There is a marked movement within Pentecostal ranks away from fundamentalism toward a more polished and sophisticated theology with a continuing emphasis on charismatic gifts.

In *Racing Toward 2001,* Russell Chandler points to the importance of the Pentecostal movement for traditional mainstream African American religion. Says Chandler:

> As the century nears an end, there are signs that people of color are once again at the forefront of a wave of spiritual power. A new survey of America's black congregations reveals

that black Americans will increasingly look to forms of Pentecostalism for spiritual vitality. Sometime in the 21st century...half of all black church goers will be Pentecostals.[21]

The rise of pentecostalism, when seen in light of what appears to be the unavoidable death of denominationalism, clearly reflects a relentless, inexorable process of change. This is a change which cannot be avoided. This is a change which must be embraced as the foundation of what I believe will become a new ecclesiology for the Black Church.

Third. White Pulpit/Black Pew

Of recent note is the number of black or mixed congregations which are pastored and controlled by white clergy. In many instances, white clergy have amassed astounding ministries that rely primarily on the financial resources and numerical strength typically reserved for traditional black churches and black preachers. One cannot help but wonder if this development represents but another example of a kind of neo-slavery for a significant segment of African Americans. These churches are typically run by white ministers and their families with only token representation of blacks in decision-making positions. The worship style of these churches is livelier than the typically staid Euro-American worship, but often lacks the soulful sounds and cadences of Black worship. A visitor to these *interracial* churches will find a new hymnody and *praise worship* clearly influenced by white evangelical Protestantism.

The full impact of this White Pulpit/Black Pew phenomenon remains to be seen. As African American worshippers increasingly move from inner-cities to suburban communities and seek family- and service-oriented churches, this conservative white pentecostal worship and style of congregational life is swiftly becoming a popular choice.

Fourth. Whatever Happened to Black Preaching?

Historically, preaching among African Americans has been an art form studied and analyzed as much for its artistry and poetry as for its structure and content. In fact, church historians attribute the growth and vitality of the Black church in large measure to the power of Black preaching. Increasingly, however, we hear a new

---

[21] Chandler, Russell, *Racing Toward 2001*, Grand Rapids, MI: Zondervan Publishing House, 1992.

didactic form of Black preaching, a departure from the traditional prose on parade. Black *preaching* has now become Black *teaching*. Within the African American church, perhaps the most well-known articulator of this form is the Reverend Frederick K. C. Price of Los Angeles, California. Black *teaching* typically emphasizes a gospel of personal fulfillment and economic prosperity rather than the proclamation of a social gospel. In this mode the sanctuary is literally turned into a classroom. The pulpit is abandoned for an in-the-aisle, up-close and personal, verse-by-verse, exegetical repetitive style of delivery. Those who flock to their seats are busily taking notes, *hungry* for the Word.

If narrative preaching is to continue as the mainstay of black homiletics it will be increasingly important for seminaries to alter their curriculum to insure that their graduates are sound Biblical expositors. I am convinced, however, that the historical preaching form must not be abandoned. Make no mistake about it, I want to continue to stand in the well-worn path of homiletic history. There is no substitute for preaching. Paul said that "it pleased God by the foolishness of preaching to save them that believe." (1 Corinthians 1:21b).

But not only has Black preaching changed, but the Black preacher has changed as well. Gone are the days when the Black preacher was the person in the community who had the most education, was *the* role model, and around whom every civic and social event was planned. Now the Black preacher must compete for significant and responsible positions of leadership within the African American community with other black professionals. Simply having *Rev.* before your name no longer automatically gains you respect; these days you have to get it the old fashioned way and *earn* it!

IV. TURMOIL IN THE TOY BOX

In his classic writing to the Church at Corinth, the Apostle Paul speaks of the characteristics of his childhood and then goes on to suggest that as a consequence of his newly found maturity in Christ he has "put away childish things." Unfortunately, many in our churches have yet to follow Paul's example—the internal workings of our religious organizations have become *toys* and the church, quite literally, has become their *toy box!* The African American Church is marked by dissension and division that can only be called childish! And whenever children play there is usually trouble over the toys or, as I like to call it, turmoil in the toy box. But this *child's play* is anything but trivial. The struggles in this *child's play* can forecast either life or death for the African American Church in the third millennium. In my view, there are at least three kinds of turmoil in the toy box.

First. Women in Ministry

Clearly, the first kind of turmoil has to do with women in ministry. In 1994 this issue is yet as divisive as ever. Some of my brothers in ministry would dare defile the Word of God with such spurious notions as: "if God had wanted women to be preachers, God would have made one of them a disciple." Some would exclude women from the pulpit by using a biased interpretation of selected Pauline passages. Referring to both Paul and Jesus, J. Deotis Roberts addresses this issue in his latest work, *The Prophethood of Black Believers:*

> The black church is burdened by conflict in its unclear understanding of the appropriate arrangements for wholesome male-female relationships....The issue is not whether black women accept an inferior status or role; it is, rather, whether they ought to lay claim to that which is theirs by God-given right as Christians who are equal to men in creation and through grace....Sexism is a sin against grace just as it is a sin against creation. The author of creation is also the giver of grace. Men as human beings do not have the right to interpose their wills over against God's purpose in creation or redemption.[22]

Let me be candid here. In my view, Roberts is too kind. Those who participate in this process of gender exclusion are guilty of ecclesiastical chicanery, egotistical elitism, and baptized bigotry.

The last time I checked, man was not in charge of the calling process. It is God who calls and we who answer. God is not interested in petty matters of sex or gender. God's work is not confined to masculinity or femininity. God reserves the right to be God. God does not require input into His decision-making process. God's Spirit is poured out on *all flesh.* When three-fourths of those who fill our pews and our offering plates are women, when those who carry the burden for the ministries—and for the pots and pans—are

---

[22] Roberts, J. Deotis, *The Prophethood of Black Believers,* Louisville, KY: Westminster/John Knox Press, 1994, pp. 81-82.

women, when those who put the Ferragamo shoes on our feet and the silk suits on our backs are women, how dare we or anyone stand in the face of God and say women can't preach? I much prefer Paul's final word on the matter of religious exclusivity: "There is neither Jew nor Greek, there is neither bond nor free, there is neither male nor female: for ye are all one in Christ Jesus!" (Galatians 3:28)

Second. Dealing with the S word!

Hopefully, one day soon the African American Church will come to deal seriously and meaningfully with the "s" word—sex. The whole arena of human sexuality, its implications and its complications, is still taboo in far too many African American Churches. This is serious business to which the Church must attend. It is time—past time—for us to take off the robes of our pseudoreligiosity and get down to the issues which are of life and death moments for the people whom we serve.

We need to talk about human sexuality in the Church. We need to talk about abortion, abstinence, adultery, fornication, masturbation, lesbianism and homosexuality. We must come to grips with the implications of AIDS and other sexually transmitted diseases for the African American community. These are issues which must be discussed freely and openly. Enlightenment must begin in the Church because many of our members are still unable to freely discuss with their children the awesome beauty and responsibility of human sexuality.

Some suggest that this generation will not be restricted by the sexual values of previous generations. Some distinguished clerics have suggested that in Cornel West's *post-modern* world we have reached the point where we need to redefine basic sexual rules. Some theologians have posited that in light of our Adamic nature, we now have license to take unto ourselves the responsibility and free will for the shaping of our own sexual values. We are enjoined to construct and interpret our values and mores in light of our own contextual experience.

But that's why we're in the mess we're in now. This notion of situational Biblical interpretation is nothing new. Men and women have always wanted to make the scripture say what they wanted it to say. The sons and daughters of Adam and Eve are always interested in placing limitations and conditions on God's right to be God.

Sin always wants to conform scripture to its own psychological and physical needs.

Quite candidly, the problem that the African American Church faces is one of its own creation. The moral preachments of those who stand in black pulpits have already alienated hundreds and thousands who are no longer convinced that they can come within the walls of the traditional church for the nurturing they need, the comfort they require or the grace which God has guaranteed. At the same time, those who preach *the whole counsel of God*—a view that is not culturally popular—fear that they will be branded as homophobic, judgmental, and insensitive.

On the other hand, the Gospel as I understand it suggests that the Church is not here to *condone* the culture but to *redeem and convert* the culture to the way of Christ. If our preaching has power, it has the power to produce changed lives. God did not make sex bad; God made it a fulfilling and life-producing moment of incredible beauty and joy.

The preacher in me says that we must aid those we pastor whose lifestyles are not consistent with our understanding of Biblical principles toward a changed life. There is no need to preach if we strip from the Gospel its converting, redeeming, restorative power. We must never exclude those whose choices are different from our own, but we must never fail them by denying the power of the Gospel to secure dignity, self-respect, and self-esteem. The Church must make a choice. The Church must decide to be faithful to its commission and calling in order that the Beloved Community is also a Redeemed Community.

If the Church takes no stand on moral issues like homosexuality, AIDS, teenage pregnancy, abortion, and sexually transmitted diseases, we will have allowed God's Word to be revised and reshaped by a culture out of control. Sexual behavior that contradicts scripture, whether heterosexual or homosexual, will result in spiritual death. We have in our hands the means and mode of our own genocide.

Unless we come to a sense of God's purpose in human sexuality we will arrive at a day like that when Hezekiah sent a word to Isaiah:

This is a day of trouble, and of rebuke, and blasphemy: for the children are come to the birth, and there is not strength to bring forth. (Isaiah 37:3)

As Dr. Cheryl Sanders from the faculty here at the Howard Divinity School has said with power and clarity, we must make our children a present priority in the African American Church. Our children must be the embodiment of the solution to our present crisis. They are expecting something from us, but they have come to the birth and there is not strength to bring forth. They are caught in the birth canal of human history—stuck in a passage of psychosexual ambiguity and ethical contradiction. There is no strength to bring forth.

Third. Stimulation Addiction

There can be little argument that most of the decline and decay in our society comes as a direct result of some form of addictive behavior. We seek to be constantly stimulated rather than to live in the harmony of oneness with the Lord whose creative handiwork we are.

Strangely enough, we are addicted to stimulation even in the church. Too often, instead of teaching or inspiring or organizing for collective growth, the church is providing entertainment to those in need of a stimulation fix. They come to the church for their weekly *dose* of gospel music, their *shouting* bearing a remarkable resemblance to the experience of *overdose*—from an incredible euphoria to rhythmic convulsions and loss of consciousness!

There has been a rapid and precipitous shift in the music expression of worship within the African American church. Dr. Wyatt Tee Walker of the Canaan Baptist Church in Harlem suggests that one can always detect what Blacks are experiencing sociologically by listening to what is being said through the music of the church. It is clear that the standard hymns of the Church are being lost; there is little interest in the classical anthems of the church; and even the Negro Spiritual is not appreciated by this generation of worshippers. In order to gain acceptance, music must be rhythmical, supported by electric instrumentation, drums, tambourines, and concert-quality sound systems. Choirs must be gowned in bright and extravagant robes, sway as they sing and from time to time resort to choreography as a means of gaining audience participation and response.

Perhaps I am one of only a few who care, but I think something disastrous is afoot when our children cannot sing "Jesus Keep Me Near the Cross," or when the contemporary Gospel—quite obviously the music of choice—has no theological moment or merit. Mind you, I have nothing against the gospel idiom. I simply believe we have lost the balance which has for generations been characteristic of African American worship, in favor of stimulation for the sake of stimulation alone.

I do not suggest diluting our authentic expression of worship, which naturally evokes both a verbal and expressive witness. For centuries within the African American Church experience, our people have shared a joyous release from anxieties and tensions through music, freeing them from any need to rely upon external stimulants. While we must avoid the temptation to create *orgasmic* worship through music, our ability to shout in the midst of a society gone insane sustains our psychospiritual health. But a steady diet of worship experience and musical expression that stimulate without enriching and nourishing, like an addictive drug, will result in nothing less than psychological and spiritual death.

But let us keep these questions and controversies which plague the church in clear perspective. Perhaps, as Frank Crane points out, we need to take a longer view:

> In the age-long disputes of the Church...as far as I can read, not one of them were ever settled anyhow. They were good fights and lasted for centuries but every one of them seemed to be a draw. Almost all the theological disputes that have been settled at all have been settled by outgrowing and forgetting them. If there are no longer any heated discussions on the great questions [facing the church] it is not because either set of champions proved their point but because nobody cares anymore. Neither side won the game; the spectators left the benches. As a matter of fact almost all the theological points that have been the storm centers of contention have really had no relation to life, and by and large the people found it out.[23]

Interestingly, Crane's comment was made in 1928. The problems which the Church faces in 1994 are not those which have no relation to life. They are problems, however, which our members seem to have resolved for themselves by either deserting the traditional church or ignoring the doctrines and dictums of the church. The spectators are quickly leaving the benches. Should the Church ignore this reality it will do so to its own peril.

[23] Crane, Frank, *Why I am a Christian*, New York: Wm. H. Wise & Company, 1928, p.29.

V. THE PROMISE OF HIS PRESENCE

What then shall we say to these things? If, indeed, these are days of social upheaval and revolutionary change, where then is hope? If the challenges before the church are so numerous as to be overwhelming where shall we begin and where shall we end? If we believe that the church at the close of the twentieth century has become *slick, manipulative and marketable,* shall we pronounce her *dead on arrival* and send for the *Joseph of Arimathaea Undertaking Company* to come and place the corpse in an available tomb? If the assessment of this hour is that we are struggling with cultural intrusion and ecclesiastical erosion and turmoil in the toy box, is our faith futile and is our hope in vain?

Well, last night I discussed the matter with Jesus. And He reminded me of that moment after his confrontation with the religious aristocracy, after his altercation with the political power structure, after he had dealt with the socio-economic problems of the time. All He said was, "The foxes have holes, the birds have nests but the Son of Man hath nowhere to lay His head." (Matthew 8:20)

I talked to Jesus about this church situation and He reminded me that after they beat Him all night Thursday night, lynched Him on Friday, and kept Him in a cold tomb 'til Sunday morning; after the resurrection, after the stone was rolled away, after the empty tomb was discovered, doubting disciples confronted, and weeping women comforted, somebody heard Him say, "I am the resurrection and the life!" (John 11:25)

I talked to Jesus about the future of the Black Church and He reminded me of that moment after breakfast on the beach, after He told Peter to "feed the sheep," after he held a meeting with 500 brethren at once, after He put His foot on a cloud bound from earth to glory, He turned around long enough to say, "All power is given unto me in heaven and in earth...and, lo, I am with you alway, even unto the end of the world." (Matthew 28:18-20)

You can go from Jerusalem, to Samaria, to Judea and to the uttermost parts of the earth because I am with you.

I'm with you in good times and in bad.

I'm with you in sunshine and in shadow.

I'm with you on the mountain high or in the valley low.

I'm with you when your world is turned upside down.

I'm with you when it looks like the bottom has fallen out.

I'm with you alway, even...!

I conclude where I began. Don't give up on the Church. I haven't given up on the Church. For all its failures and faults I still believe it's His Church. Don't give up on the Church. The gates of hell shall not prevail against it. It's the only thing He's coming back for. Don't give up on the church.

Fear not; I am with thee;
O be not dismayed!
For I am thy God,
and will still give thee aid;
I'll strengthen thee, help thee, and cause thee to stand,
Upheld by my gracious, omnipotent hand.

The soul that on Jesus
hath leaned for repose,
I will not, I will not
desert to his foes;
That soul, though all hell should endeavor to shake,
I'll never, no, never, no never forsake![24]

---

[24] How Firm A Foundation, George Keith, Baptist Standard Hymnal.

CHAPTER TEN

The Pregnancy of God

Opening Remarks on the occasion of the entry into the
new offices of the National Council of Negro Women in
Washington, District of Columbia on December 18, 1995

To the Honorable Dorothy Height, Attorney Dovey Roundtree, Mrs. Brenda Girton Mitchell, Members of the Board of Directors, distinguished visitors and honored guests:

I am awed by the high honor of being permitted to share in this opening ceremony of the new offices of the National Council of Negro Women. This is, indeed, an historic moment...a moment which must live in the hearts and minds of all African American women and men.

Visions are hard to come by. Dreams rarely come true. We are met today in that special moment when the vision of woman becomes consonant with the will and purpose of God. It is a rare moment, indeed, when human purposes are kissed by divine benediction.

This is a rare moment when the ancestors applaud from the battlements of heaven and when generations yet unborn leap in the womb of anticipation and hope.

This is a rare moment when this new Sojourner named *Dorothy* speaks of freedom in more excellent tones, and this new Harriet named *Height* leads the women of her race to this last stop on the underground railway.

This is a rare moment when the signs are unmistakable, when the signals are irrefutable, when the whole world can see that from this place, a generation of tall, proud African American women will rise and lead!

I am aware that this day has been long in coming. Plans had been made to stand in this place long before now. But I think it is providential that we meet in this hour, in this season of celebration of the birth of the Christ, He who would be Savior of the world. It clearly speaks, however, of the adventures of a woman...a young woman...a pregnant young woman, afraid, frightened and alone in a male dominated world.

Yet the story of Mary serves only to point the way to a deeper, more abiding truth. If the nativity narrative means anything at all, it means that God is doing something that God has never done before, God is speaking in a way that God has never spoken before, and God is moving in the affairs of God's people in a way that God has never moved before.

While it may not seem so, the Bethlehem story is not about angels, it is not about Joseph, it is not really about Mary. It is a story about God. What it really speaks to is what I call *The Pregnancy of God.*

How dare I speak of the pregnancy of God? If you're offended by the notion, maybe it's because we've limited our thinking about God to the gender-specific, failing to acknowledge that God is what God needs to be, whenever God needs to be whatever God needs to be. Because God is OMNIpotent, it means that God is never IMpotent. Not only do I suggest that God is pregnant, but in point of fact, that God is the fountain and source of God's own impregnation.

God is always pregnant.

When the world is nothing but a wasteless abyss, God is pregnant with creation.

When Abraham could provide no lodging place for his seed, God was pregnant in the womb of a woman named Sarah.

When the children of Israel were caught in a system of violent and abusive slavery, God became pregnant in a woman named Jochebed.

When the people of Israel had no voice to announce the coming of the Messiah, Zechariah became speechless at the thought but God became pregnant in a woman named Elisabeth.

When the world needed a Savior, when the world needed a wonderful Counselor, a mighty God, an everlasting Parent and a Prince of Peace, God didn't use Herod, God didn't use wise men, God didn't use Shepherds, God didn't use Joseph—God was God all by God's Self and God became pregnant in a woman named Mary.

And the scriptures teach us that Mary delivered when the time was accomplished. Birth took place when the moment was right.

God stepped down through 42 generations, as the scriptures tell us, "in the fulness of time." Down through 42 generations, God was the attending surgeon that transferred the divine essence into the realm of human flesh. "The Word became flesh," the idea of God took form, the priority of God was wrapped up in human person-ality, the purposes of God made themselves manifest not when we said so but when God said so.

We are here to celebrate not what we have done but what God has done. We are here to celebrate what we already know...that God moves in mysterious ways, His wonders to perform. We are here to celebrate what we already know...that the wheels of justice grind slow but they grind exceedingly fine. We are here to celebrate what we have already known...that the labor and blood of Sojourner, and Harriet, and Phyllis Wheatley, and Fannie Lou Hamer, and Mary McCloud Bethune, and Josephine Baker, and Wilma Rudolph, and Nannie Helen Boroughs and Ida B. Wells, and Marion Anderson, and Madam C. J. Walker, and Lorraine Hansberry, and all the other matriarchs of our race has not been spilled in vain. We are here to celebrate the very pregnancy of God!

We are not here to celebrate a building, we are here to celebrate how God has brought us from a mighty, mighty long way. We are here to celebrate that God has made a way for God's children to stand even in the midst of uncertainty and doubt. God has found a way to bring dignity even in the midst of disgrace. God has found a way to keep us marching, *bloodied but unbowed.* God has found yet another way to tell Pharoah to let His people go. God has made a way that the sisters will no longer be found waiting to exhale! God has found a way to impregnate a people with a God-ordained idea and then bring it to birth before our wondering eyes. God has found a way to take God's children—the progeny of slaves, the great grandchildren of black women torn *from* Africa and then raped *in* America, victims of every known form of man-made abuse—God has taken God's children and put them smack dab in the middle of Pennsylvania Avenue! The White House can't look around you and the Congress can't look over you.

God is doing a new thing and has allowed us to be here in this place to witness it. Thanks be to God that we are here today in that rarest of moments when the vision of woman, when the vision of this woman, when the vision of Dorothy Irene Height, when the

vision of all black women throughout the world become consonant with the will and purpose of God. Let God be thanked. Let
God be praised!

CHAPTER ELEVEN

Sometimes I Wish My Eyes Hadn't Been Opened...

❧

The First National Conference on Black Philanthropy
March 7, 1997
Philadelphia, Pennsylvania

Sometimes I wish my eyes hadn't been opened.
Sometimes I wish I could no longer see all
  of the pain and the hurt
and the longing of my people and me as we
  try to be free.
Sometimes I wish my eyes hadn't been opened.
Just for a moment, how sweet it would be
not to be struggling
not to be striving
but just to sleep secretly in our slavery...

The words of this haunting soliloquy by an unknown poet speak of the pain and the pathos of the human predicament, of what it means just to struggle to be free. Strange these words seem to me...***Sometimes I wish my eyes hadn't been opened.***

Those of my generation and beyond share with me a nostalgia for the days of our innocence and youth. It is not that they were *the good old days*. Some of those days clearly were not good. But they were days of simplicity, days when life moved in a steady routine, days when a barefoot boy could beat his feet in Louisiana mud and think he was having a great time.

I remember those days; I remember my childhood in the south: I remember the ordinary joy of going to the corner store for a *Nehi* grape or an *RC Cola*, or picking up a loaf of *Sunbeam* or *Holsum* bread for Mama Gladys. I remember when there were no video games, or CD's, or *MTV* or computers or the Internet.

But I *was* entertained in those days by swinging on a rope swing in the school yard, trying with all my might to touch the clouds with my toes. I was entertained in those days just walking along the road to my Grandfather's house, waiting for old Buicks and rusted out Chevy's to come by with dust flying a mile in their wake. I was entertained by picking wild blackberries which would soon show up baked in a cobbler on a warm summer's eve. It was such a simple and innocent time. But now, *sometimes I wish my eyes hadn't been opened.*

I am a child of Louisiana by birth, born in an era of the Second World War, when black Americans were still called *Negroes,* or *colored.* My mores, my perceptions of the world, my understanding of who I was and what I could become were shaped and molded by the era which preceded the civil rights movement.

I can remember a day in my life when I had more aunts and uncles than I could count, most of whom had no connection with me by birth or by blood but who were joined to me by a connection rooted somewhere in the soul.

I remember a day gone by when we knew—*Once when we were colored*—who we were and that we had something to uphold. We may have been poor and lacking some material things, but our mothers and our grandmothers and aunties saw to it that we went to school with clothes clean, hair combed and faces greased down. We knew what it was to be the only family on our block to have a television and to have the whole neighborhood gather up to see Ezzard Charles, Jersey Joe Walcott, and Sugar Ray Robinson fight for the race on the Wednesday night *Gillette* Cavalcade of Stars.

To look sharp and be on the ball,
to feel sharp every time you call,
to stay sharp
use Gillette Blue Blades for the
quickest, slickest shave of all!

But those days are gone now....*Sometimes I wish my eyes hadn't been opened.*

And now here we are—fully mature, responsible representatives of the religious, political, social, economic and philanthropic communities. We are here, or so we think, because we are the ones who've made it, those who have *arrived.* Try as we might to avoid it, however, reality yields a frightening sobriety. This is a moment when our nation is struggling toward the end of one century in search of meaning for the next. It is a moment when the social order is neither social nor orderly, when the need for new leadership at every level of our common life cries out from the soil beneath our feet. This is a moment when the great issues of our time are more ethical than economic and when the hope of our time rests more with things spiritual than with things physical.

I would not speak to this significant assemblage with cynicism or despair, but yet there is something deep within me that cries out: ***Sometimes I wish my eyes hadn't been opened.***

Don't look now but racism is still alive and well in America. In the *land of the free and the home of the brave,* racism has dressed up in the robes of religion. The Newt Gingrich's of the world are where they are because the politics of race are baptized by religious conservatives and spread abroad by the political right.

Don't look now but it would appear that we have citizenship in a land where the gap between rich and poor increases daily, where affordable housing is a commodity too few can afford and many will never attain, where the public schools have been abandoned by all except those who have no alternative, where decent health care is available only to those who can afford it, and where insurance companies practice medicine in pursuit of profits.

Like it or not, we are a part of a society that cares everything about *volume* and nothing about *values.* We live our lives among those who celebrate *quantity* but who quickly forsake *quality.* Ours is a day when *much* is always preferred over *little,* and when what you *have* is more important than what you *are.* ***Sometimes I wish my eyes hadn't been opened.***

And yet, there ought be lessons. There ought be lessons transmitted from one generation to the other. There ought be lessons that serve as platforms of dignity and pride upon which our children and our children's children can stand. There ought be lessons—taught by Martin, and Medgar, and Malcolm—which can stand the test of time and provide firm footing for the paths of new leadership.

If there is a word chiseled into my brain, it is a word given to me by my father. When I was growing up, whenever my father would take me somewhere he would always say:

Don't forget who you are;

Don't forget where you've come from.

It is important to know who you are. When the world tries to define you, it is important to know who you are. You cannot know who you are, however, unless you first know from whence you have come. If, as Martin King has suggested, our destiny is bound up in a "garment of mutuality," then I cannot forget where I came from.

I know I came from the kingdoms of Africa on the other side of the Atlantic. I know where I came from.

I know that if there were an Adam and Eve and a Garden of Eden, they weren't found in Europe. They would have been in Kenya, where anthropologists say the oldest remains of human beings are to be found. I know where I came from.

I am a descendant of the Moors who brought Europe out of the Dark Ages and ushered in the Renaissance. I am not of the lineage of Hippocrates, whom some say is the Father of Medicine; I am a descendent of Imhotep who laid the foundation for medicine, pyramid building, military strategy, philosophy and poetry. I know where I came from.

My history was forged on the backs of your ancestors and mine; a history of fields we tilled but did not own, of food we cooked but could not eat, of houses we cleaned but in which we could not reside. My history is a history of grandmothers who were raped, great grandfathers who were castrated, great aunts and uncles who were hunted down by rabid bloodhounds, of brothers who, like Emmit Till, were hung on lynching trees. I know where I came from. But *sometimes I wish my eyes hadn't been opened.*

Still there ought be lessons. There ought be lessons distilled from our past that open the door to our future. If there is a lesson which my people should have learned over the last few years it is another one of those lessons I learned as a child:

Every tub has got to sit on its own bottom.

It's an old lesson but it's still true. When government set-asides have been set aside; when affirmative action is denied; when scholarships designed to help correct the wrongs of the past are themselves declared wrong; government hand-outs are taken back; when welfare as we know it has sunk to rise no more; when nobody salutes Black Power or tells you that *Black is beautiful* anymore; when nobody is passing out reparation checks of guilt and repentance just because of the color of your skin, somebody has got to learn the lesson that every tub must sit on its own bottom.

If we have learned the lessons of the past we have learned that what we used to be must not be an excuse for our failures. Rather, it must be the badge of pride upon which we hang our future.

Yes, we were slaves but what I used to be will not define what I am going to be. Yes, we were slaves whose languages were lost, whose identities were obscured, and whose families were destroyed, but we must never fail to speak to each other, to be true to ourselves and to keep our families intact. Yes, we were slaves but we must never permit the way we were treated in the past to define the way we live today and behave tomorrow. Yes, we were slaves but the death that was around us could not destroy the life that is within us. Yes, we were slaves but God has for us a new destiny, a new identity, a new definition and a new determination. Yes, we were victims but God has made us victors.

I hear somebody saying, Wait a minute. You're a preacher. Didn't you come here to tell us what God can do?

Well, I'm glad you asked that question, because what I really came to tell you is that whatever you do and whatever you become in this world will come as a consequence of **DIVINE/HUMAN COOPERATION.**

What I came to say is that you cannot do everything for yourself but God is not going to do for you that which you can do for yourself.

God will liberate you and deliver you but you must participate in the process of your own liberation.

There are some who will tell you that the age of miracles is past. They will tell you that in the modern computerized age, miracles don't happen anymore. They will tell you that in an age of cyberspace, the Internet and the World Wide Web, there is no such thing as a miracle. But since you reminded me that I am a regularly ordained Baptist preacher I'm here to tell you that the God I serve *is* a miracle working God. But miracles come to pass because of a divine/human partnership. If there is going to be a change in our circumstances or a miracle in our lives, we've got to participate in the process.

This is the principle: God will provide the light to chase away our darkness but we must get up and go to work in God's sunshine.

When Jesus turned water into wine nobody else could change the water into wine. The bride and groom couldn't change it, Mary the mother of Jesus couldn't change it, the disciples couldn't change water into wine. The scripture says that Jesus turned the water into wine. But Jesus *did not* fill up the pots with water. That's something they could do. At the very least they could get up, go get the water and put it in the pot!

Jesus took two sardines and five biscuits and fed 5,000 not counting the women and the children. The New Testament wants us to know that only Jesus can feed 5,000 with biscuits and sardines. You can't do it, the Democrats can't do it, the Republicans can't do it, Newt Gingrich can't do it, GO-PAC can't do it, and Bill Clinton can't do it. Only Jesus can feed the multitudes with biscuits and sardines.

After the meal was over, however, he told them to get 12 baskets and pick up what was left. Now, listen. If Jesus could multiply biscuits and sardines He also had the power to clean up after the meal. But He will not do for you what you can do for yourself. If there is some cleaning up to be done in our neighborhoods we've got to do it for ourselves.

God has something for us, but we must work for it. It must come through divine/human cooperation.

I tell the young people in my church that God has a job for you but God won't look in the paper for you, or write a resume for you, or go to the interview for you.

God will get you into Howard, and Harvard, and Penn State, and into law school and medical school. But God won't study for you or write term papers for you or go to class for you. You've got to do that for yourself.

Frederick Douglass was right: "In this world you may not get everything you work for, but you must certainly work for everything you get." God is still in the miracle business. God can still change men and nations. God can still change individuals and institutions. But God won't do for you what you must do for yourself. Miracles come as a consequence of a divine/human cooperation.

We are gathered in this conference on Black Philanthropy because the day for excuses is over. It is true that we live in a racist society and racism still speaks.

So, Let racism reverse every gain won during the civil rights movement.

Let racism tell you that the only place for black men is in jail.

Let racism tell you that building prisons for our children to die in is better than building colleges and universities for our children to learn in.

Let racism tell you that our children choose to be drug addicts when we don't own any boats, we don't own any planes, we don't own the means of production nor permit the distribution.

Let racism tell you that black politicians are not to be trusted, so the democratic right of a people to control their own destiny must be handed over to appointed overseers.

Ah, but if we lay the fault for all our problems at the feet of racism we will have missed the point. There are some things which God will straighten out but before He does, there are some things we must straighten out for ourselves. The truth of the matter is that nobody can hurt us like we can hurt us and nobody can rip black folk off like black folk. It's time to stop blaming others for problems and take responsibility for ourselves.

But still, *Sometimes I wish my eyes hadn't been opened.*

Still, there ought be lessons. Can't you hear the lessons? I hear the lessons. Somebody's teaching a lesson.

What's the lesson, **HARRIET TUBMAN?** You were caught in the web of slavery but you took those who were lost from the land of slavery to the land of freedom and forever you have been known as the *Moses* of your people.

What's the lesson, **SOJOURNER TRUTH?** Yes, you were black as the midnight sun but you refused to let others deny your womanhood. In 1851 you stood up in the Women's Rights Convention and asked the world: *"Ain't I a woman?"*

What's the lesson, **MALCOLM X?** Yes, you were misunderstood in your day. We didn't believe you when told us that the system could not be trusted. We didn't trust you when you told us the truth about our history, when you told us how to empower black people. We didn't believe you when you declared that black people would have to fight for their rights *by any and all means necessary.* But if we didn't believe you then, we sure believe you now.

What's the lesson, **MARTIN KING?** Yes, you were a black preacher from the South but you stood before Bull Connor and Jim

Clark. You wrote letters from a Birmingham jail. You electrified a nation standing on the steps of the Lincoln Monument. You taught black folk how to kneel in prayer and rise in power. So,

Now we don't just ride the bus, we own the bus...

Now we don't just clean the hotels, we own the hotels...

Because you died one day in Memphis there are black mayors in City Halls, black judges on our bench, black men and women in the House and a black woman in the Senate.

Don't you hear the lesson? Don't you go around here talking about how you made it on your own. Don't you go around here talking about how you pulled yourself up by your own bootstraps. Before you got where you are you didn't have any bootstraps because you didn't have any boots. And some of us can remember a time when we didn't have any shoes. That's why we started singing, *I got shoes, you got shoes...when I get to heaven I'm gonna put on my shoes...* because we didn't have any shoes down here.

I know you are a Black Philanthropist; I know you are a mover and a shaker; I know you represent the money centers of corporate America; I know you make decisions on how to spend other people's money and your own, but the lesson is: never forget that you are where you are today because somebody prayed for you before you knew how to pray for yourself. Somebody marched for you. Somebody suffered for you. Somebody sacrificed for you. Somebody scrubbed floors for you. Somebody bled and died for you. And now that you're in here dining on china with a linen napkin in your lap don't you forget to return to the land from which you came and make something out of someone else.

Ah, but still, *Sometimes I wish my eyes hadn't been opened.*

And there are lessons yet to be learned. The social politics of the past would suggest to us that African Americans are economically deprived and politically impoverished. I make bold to suggest, however, that our real poverty is not a deficit of money but a poverty of the spirit. Our greatest poverty is in the deficit of our children who are more afraid of living than they are of dying, who spend more time planning their funerals than they do planning their lives. I do not expect to be popular when I leave here today but let me tell you it's time to move to a higher plane, to a new dimension of living where the dignity of all is affirmed.

If our generation learns anything at all from our ancestors it ought to be that we can be who we are, without excuses. I may not have everything I want, but I can be who I am. I may not be who others think I ought to be but I can be who God wants me to be.

Who I am is not determined by the cut of my hair.

Who I am is not determined by the Kente cloth I wear.

Who I am is not determined by my touchdown pass, my home run hit or my slam dunk.

Who I am is not determined by Reebok, Nike or Michael Jordan.

And who I am to become will not be determined by *Ebonics,* or by *black English* or any of the rest of this foolishness. Let me assure you that I understand the purpose of calling *Ebonics* another language. Properly understood *Ebonics* is an African American variant of what we call *standard English.* It is an acknowledgment of an entire language system in the streets that is experienced across the country. While I acknowledge that some educators view the use of *Ebonics* as a strategy for teaching English, I reject what I regard as a dangerous methodology even if it is viewed as a means toward a more purposeful end.

Let me say it in plain English:

- I'll teach my children *Ebonics* when they change "i before e except after c or when sounded like a, as in neighbor and weigh."
- I'll teach my children *Ebonics* when they teach *Ebonic* math, and *Ebonic* chemistry, and *Ebonic* medicine.
- I'll teach my children *Ebonics* when *USA Today* and the *Washington Post* permit split infinitives and dangling modifiers.
- I'll teach my children *Ebonics* when *A E I O U* and sometimes *Y* becomes *I be, you be, we be* in *U.S. News and World.*

Don't be fooled. It's another trick. Don't believe the hype.

If our history has taught us anything at all it is that we must stand on the high ground of excellence. This is not the time to lower our standards, it is the time to raise our standards. This is not the time to excuse the tragedy of public education by pointing to what is common among us; this is the time to rise above our limitations and set our sights on those things which the world believes are beyond us.

Sometimes I wish my eyes hadn't been opened but then I thank God that they have been. My eyes are open enough to know that the secret of life is not in what we have but in who we are. Whoever you are, from whatever station of life you have come, despite the obstacles which may have been in your path, beyond any victories you have earned on your own, I have come to tell you to OPEN YOUR EYES!

God has given you the vision to see beyond the moment and the ability to set an example and agenda for our people.

Open your eyes.

God has given you a healthy self-assurance and strength of character which will help secure the future for generations yet unborn.

Open your eyes.

God has given you—strong progeny of our race—tongues to articulate the history of our ancestors. You must articulate who we are and what we must become as much by the pride that is in your eyes, the dignity that is in your walk, and the excellence that is in your work, as by the words you speak with your mouth.

Open your eyes.

The poet wrote:

Sometimes I wish my eyes hadn't been opened.
Sometimes I wish I could no longer see all
of the pain and the hurt
and the longing of my people and me as we
try to be free.
Sometimes I wish my eyes hadn't been opened.
Just for a moment, how sweet it would be
not to be struggling
not to be striving
but just to sleep secretly in our slavery...

However, the poet didn't stop there:

But now that I've seen with my eyes I can't
close them
Because deep inside me somewhere I'd still
know
The road my people and I have to travel,
My heart would say Yes, and my feet would say, Go.

Sometimes I wish my eyes hadn't been opened
But now that they have I'm determined to see
that somehow my people and I, this day
will be the people that God created us to be.

OPEN UP YOUR EYES!

CHAPTER TWELVE

A Strange Path
to Power!

༺⚘༻

*T*hen Samuel took the horn of oil, and anointed him in the midst of
his brethren: and the Spirit of the Lord came upon David from that
day forward. So Samuel rose up and went to Ramah. (1 Samuel 16:13)
And David rose up early in the morning, and left the sheep with a
keeper, and took, and went, as Jesse had commanded him. (1 Samuel
17:20a)

Within the crucible of the sacred writings we know as the Old
Testament, there is no personality who dominates the landscape
more forcefully than does a young man named David. No matter
how one views him, his was a life marked by tragedy and triumph,
by dignity and disgrace, by pain and passion. So important was
this David, that Israel's history and his history would be forever
intertwined.

Scour the record books of history and in David you will find both
warrior and womanizer, eloquent poet and exquisite musician, a
treacherous friend and a passionate lover, a leader of praise, a tender of sheep, a sinner for whom there was no peer and one, whom
the ages will affirm, was a man after God's own heart.

The book of Samuel is, as you know, the record of the prophetic work of Israel's last judge. It is a book of *great beginnings and
tragic endings.* Most importantly, however, the Book of Samuel is
the revealed record which shares much of the life of this *sweet
singer of Israel.* This book marks the days of Israel moving from a
theocracy—when God ruled—to a monarchy, when men ruled.
This book speaks not only of David's time, but it speaks as well of
what I have come to call a strange path to power.

If perchance you do not recall the circumstances of this text, I
need only remind you that Saul was King in Israel. Saul, however,

because of jealousy, superstition, and an ego that was out of control, had fallen out of favor with God. At the time of our text, then, God has determined to choose a king for Israel from among the eight sons of one Jesse, a Bethlehemite. From the moment that Samuel shows up on Jesse's doorstep, there ensues a long process of determining who among his sons will be invested with the power of the royal office and be anointed king in Israel.

One by one, the sons of Jesse stand before Samuel. First, Eliab, then Abinadab, then Shammah and all the rest.

There they were. Strong, virile, young men.

There they were with impressive resumes in their hands.

There they were, dressed for success, degrees tightly clutched in their hands.

There they were, jockeying to impress others with who they were and what they had to offer.

No doubt, Samuel and his retinue were impressed with what they saw. But this book says that every time Samuel thought he had the next king God said, *No, Samuel. What you're seeing is something that's external but what I'm looking for is something that's internal. I'm not worried about what he's got on him; I'm worried about what he's got in him. No, Samuel.* "Man looketh on the outward appearance, but the Lord looketh on the heart." (1 Samuel 16:7)

From the sheepfold comes the last of Jesse's sons. He's the youngest boy. The runt of the litter. The one that's still wet behind the ears. Scripture says he has a ruddy complexion and a handsome appearance. He's the one that nobody pays much attention to because he spends all of his time tending sheep and playing harps.

But when Samuel sees him there is no doubt that this is the one.

This is the one upon whose shoulders the mantle of leadership shall rest.

This is the one who shall lead his people in war and in peace.

This is the one upon whose head an earthly crown shall be placed.

This is the one in whose hand shall be given the scepter of human power.

"And the Lord said, Arise, anoint him; for this is he." (1 Samuel 16:12)

There is no debate about it, this is the one. And the scripture says that David was blessed, set apart, consecrated. David was anointed to be King in Israel. That's what it says. In the sixteenth chapter and the thirteenth verse, Samuel took the horn of oil and, in the presence of his brothers, anointed David to be King.

However, that's not the end of the story. In the seventeenth chapter of the same book it says that David was back in the field tending sheep. In the seventeenth chapter and the twentieth verse, David leaves his sheep early in the morning. Maybe you didn't understand. In the sixteenth chapter, God said David is supposed to be the King. In the sixteenth chapter, David is anointed King. But in the seventeenth chapter, David is still tending sheep.

There's something wrong with this picture. If I understand this moment in the life of David correctly, he who was taken from the pasture was anointed to be King and was then sent back to the pasture. I don't understand it. It does not appear to be in the character of God to perform such a cosmic slight of hand. It looks like it's unfair. I don't mean to interrogate God but I do have a question. Why did God give David the idea that the kingdom was his and then send him back to the pasture? Why did God bless David's life with the oil of anointment and then send him back to the pasture? Why did God hold him up as the one in whom He would place authority and power, only to send him back to the pasture he came from?

Now, I cannot be certain, but this text seems to suggest that in between where you are and where you want to be, there is always some *PASTURE TIME.*

It looks like in between the time you get the degree in your hand and the time when you arrive at the position to which you are destined, there's some *pasture time.* I realize this is the day somebody was supposed to tell you that you've got it made; somebody was to tell you that you have arrived at the place to which you know you were entitled. I really don't want to disappoint you, but between the time you walk across this platform and the time you get that promotion you've been looking for, I might as well be honest with you, you've got some *pasture time* coming.

May I take the time to tell you that it's in the *pasture time* that God does God's work?

God intended to make *NOAH* the head of His reconstruction project. God intended to give Noah charge over the re-creation of the universe, but first Noah had to spend some time as the Head

Superintendent cleaning out the bottom of a floating zoo. THAT'S PASTURE TIME.

God intended for *JOSEPH* to be the Secretary of Agriculture in the administration of the Egyptian Pharaoh. God intended for Joseph to be in charge of Food Stamps when famine broke out in Israel, but before Joseph could get to his intended assignment God sent him to a pit in order to get him ready for the palace. THAT'S PASTURE TIME.

God intended for *MOSES* to be the liberator of His people. God intended for Moses to tell Pharaoh to let His people go, but before God could use him the way He intended to use him, He had to send him to the back side of Sinai. God had to send him to a place where he could see only God's back parts when His glory passed by. God had to put him on sabbatical leave before He could find any use for him. THAT'S PASTURE TIME.

Pasture time is the time when God gets your attention.

Pasture time is the time when God can talk to you and you can talk to God.

Pasture time is the time when God teaches lessons that only God can teach.

Pasture time is the time when you can hear a small voice say: "Be still and know that I am God." (Psalm 46:10)

Pasture time is the time when God builds up your courage to face giants.

Pasture time is the time when God gives instructions on how to walk through the valley and the shadow of death.

Pasture time is the time when God gives tutorials on self-defense, 'cause "No weapon that is formed against you shall prosper." (Isaiah 54:17)

Pasture time is the time when God deals with your fears: "He that dwelleth in the secret place of the most high shall abide under the shadow of the Almighty." (Psalm 91:1)

Pasture time is the time when God teaches you to handle your tears because "weeping may endure for a night but joy cometh in the morning." (Psalm 30:5)

I do not mean to be offensive today but there is a reason why David needed to go back to the pasture. David needed to go back to the pasture because *DAVID NEEDED TIME TO DEAL WITH DAVID.*

Now listen, every Sunday School child knows that David faced one obstacle and challenge after another—lions, bears, giants,

Bathsheba, Uriah and all the rest. The point of it all, however, was that David's sternest test wouldn't be external, it would be internal. David's sternest test would be David himself. The African proverb suggests:

If I can successfully negotiate the enemy within me then the enemy without can do me no harm.

When David was anointed, he was a boy who still had some growing up to do. A boy who hadn't finished maturing. David was a boy who still had to go through puberty and adolescence. God would not send a boy to do a man's job. David may have wanted power; David may have had every right to seize power because the Prophet of God had poured the oil on his head that was symbolic of power. David was anointed by God to have power. And yet, God knew that David had some growing up to do. God sent him first on a long journey, a circuitous route—a strange path to power.

Maybe what is at work here is that sometimes in pursuit of power one is required to *FOLLOW GOD WHEN YOU CAN'T SEE HIM.*

Do not forget, as you read this text, that David never questioned his *pasture time.* David never raised an objection to being returned to the lowly status of sheep tender. Understand now that after David was anointed king, he turned around and went back to the pasture. He trusted God to take him to the place he was intended to be at the time God intended for him to be there.

I realize that what I'm saying here today is strange. The scientists among us wouldn't understand it; the philosophers among us would not accept it; the intellectuals among us would want to argue about it, but I thought I ought to tell you that sometimes you have to follow God when you don't know where God is going.

And while I'm on my way, let me assure you that whatever God has designed for your life, nobody can take from you. Whatever is intended for you in the perfect will of God cannot be stripped from you. Whatever blessing God has prepared for you is yours. Nobody can steal your blessing. But you've got to trust God to bless you the way God wants you to be blessed.

If you don't know what lies ahead, that's all right. God knows.

If you don't know about your career path, that's all right. God knows.

If you don't know whether that door is going to open, that's all right. God knows.

If you don't know about your scholarship, or your fellowship, or your job opportunity, that's all right. God knows.

Stop and think about all the things you didn't know before you got to the HOUSE. Stop and think about all the questions you didn't have answers for, the tuition money you didn't have, and still don't know where it came from. God has brought you this far without any help from you. I just thought I'd tell you today that sometime you have to follow God when you don't know where God is going.

I don't know what else you learned at the HOUSE, but by now you should have learned that you can't make it by yourself. You can't make it on your intelligence alone; you can't make it because of the fraternity you joined or the friends you have; you won't make it because of the size of your bank account or because of a piece of paper that hangs on your wall.

You will come to the time in your life when you've got to trust God. There will come a time in your life when you stop looking for a reason and start looking for a relationship.

Sometime you've got to trust God when you don't know if God can be trusted.

Sometime you've got to rely on God even if you're not certain that God is reliable.

Sometime when you can't see your way you've got to trust the One who is the Way.

Sometime in your life you've got to throw your textbook out the window, throw up both your hands, and say, "Father I stretch my hand to thee, no other help I know."

If you trust Him you need to know that the blessing you need is already in His hand.

The job you need is already on the way.

That position you want, God is working it out.

The money you need is on its way to your bank account.

That problem you can't solve, God is fixing it right now.

That car you want to drive is already on the production line.

That house you want, the deed is already in your name.

And the woman you want to spend the rest of your life with is already in the HOUSE.

But you've got to trust God even when you don't know where God is going.

If you wonder what it is I'm saying today, let me be clear. David's strange path to power took him back to the pasture, required that he trust God when he could not see where God was going. And it also required that *HE NEVER FORGET HIS BROTHERS.*

Jesse, you will recall, sent David to take food to his brothers when they were in battle. Perhaps, just perhaps, the implication of this time of David's life is that no matter how high you rise, never forget your brothers. It's mighty easy to get high and mighty.

When good times come it's be easy to think you made it by yourself.

When you've got letters strung out behind your name it's easy to think the sun can't shine without your permission.

But don't forget your brothers.

Somebody else looks like you.

Somebody else has your name.

Somebody else is climbing up the rough side of the same mountain.

Don't forget your brothers.

Somebody else came from the same side of the tracks that you come from.

Somebody else has the same blood that you have.

Somebody else stayed home so you could go to school.

Somebody else prayed for you so that you could get in line today.

You didn't make it by yourself, so don't forget your brothers.

And while I'm at it, **DON'T FORGET THE SISTERS EITHER.**

I know you're on your way to positions of power and authority. I know you're on your way up the corporate ladder. I know tomorrow you'll be an entrepreneur, a surgeon, an economist. But don't forget the sisters.

Don't forget the one that made the bridge that brought you across.

Don't forget the women who worked when Daddy couldn't be found.

Don't forget the women who paid tuition by working all day and half the night.

They may be all dressed up today, but I keep on trying to tell you somebody in here worked some long hours just so you can sit where you sit.

Don't forget the sisters. They are not to be bruised. They are not to be battered. They are to be loved and respected and treated as the Nubian queens they are.

Maybe you missed the point. I keep on trying to tell you that David was anointed king in chapter 16 but he was back tending sheep in chapter 17. And maybe the point of it all is not just that we need pasture time, not just that we have to trust God when we don't know where God is going or even that we have an obligation never to forget the brothers and sisters. David went back to the pasture in order to *GET READY FOR THE GIANT.*

Now, listen. Like David, I know you're going somewhere. After all this time and all this effort, you're going somewhere. But if you thought that these four years (or five years!) in college would sweeten the ride you misunderstood the purpose of your matriculation. The only reason it was necessary for you to be here in the first place is because the giant is real.

There is a whole nation, your brothers and your sisters, your mothers and your fathers, who are counting on you to deal with the giant. The giant is real. Paul said:

> *...we wrestle not against flesh and blood,*
> *but against principalities, against powers,*
> *against the rulers of the darkness of this world,*
> *against spiritual wickedness in high places.* (Ephesians 6:12)

The giant is real. Paul said that the giant is so real that you need to "put on the whole armor of God that you may be able to stand in the evil day, and having done all, to stand." (Ephesians 6:11) The giant is real.

Chemical addiction is real.

Inadequate education is real.

Economic opression is real.

Insufficient health care is real.

There are more black men in prison than in college. That's real.

Government set-asides have been set aside. That's real.

Affirmative action is dead and buried. That's real.

Scholarships have been set back and government handouts have dried up. That's real.

Nobody salutes *Black Power* anymore.

Nobody tell you that *black is beautiful* anymore, and nobody is passing out reparation checks of guilt and repentance just because of the color of your skin. That's real.

And, whether you know it or not, racism is still very real.

I brought this to your attention because I'm led to tell you that I do not believe that Goliath was an anomaly. I believe that in the army of Philistia, Goliath was not the only giant. Goliath was just the first giant. And David's job was not to take out all the giants. David's job was just to take out this giant. If I only leave one word of challenge to you today then let it be this: Find yourself a giant and take him out!

- Wherever you find a giant that oppresses our people, take it out.
- Wherever you find a giant that robs our children of their future, take it out.
- Wherever you find a giant that attacks the very blood line of our culture and leaves us as ghastly reminders of the people God intended for us to be, take it out.
- Wherever you find a giant that more than the body enslaves the mind, take it out.

And I may as well tell you, even though the giant is real, do not fear the giant.

God has not given us the spirit of fear,
but of power and love and a strong mind. (2 Timothy 1:7)

Strong black men, do not fear the giant.

Greater is He that is in you
than he that is in the world. (John 4:4)

Do not fear the giant.

If God be for us,
who can be against us? (Romans 8:31b)

I will not tell you that the battle will not be fierce. But I'll tell you what. The only reason I do not fear the giant is because I know what God promised and I know what God did not promise.

He did not promise that I would never have danger.

But, He did promise never to leave me alone.

He did not promise that there would be no hard days, no long nights.

But He did promise to be my shield and my buckler.

He did not promise that I would never have enemies.

But He did promise that when my enemies and my foes come upon me they would stumble and fall.

He did not promise that you would not have to cry sometime.

But He did promise that He would wipe every tear from your eye.

He did not promise that the road would not be rough.

But He did promise that He would send angels to bear you up in their hands lest you dash your foot against a stone.

I believe I see it now. I believe I see why it is that David had to take this strange path to power. In fact, it's really quite clear. If I read this text properly it suggests that no matter where David was, David always understood that he was **DESTINED TO BE KING.**

In the middle of a stinking sheep pasture David knew he was destined to be king. In a place of compromise and low estate, David knew he was destined to be king.

And that's what I came to tell you today. Even in the midst of your pasture time, when you're in a dead end, cut-back, down-sized, laid-off, no-money situation don't ever forget that you are destined to be king.

When the world laughs at you just remember you are destined to be king.

When others tell you that your concepts are crazy and your ideas are idiotic, just remember you are destined to be king.

When the world tells you what you can and cannot do, just remember you are destined to be king.

Who you are, and where you are, and what you are to become is no accident. You were never intended to be ordinary. You were never intended to be pedestrian or common-place. You are destined to be king.

One of these days you will realize that:

Donald Trump is just counting your change;
Bill Gates is keeping your seat warm; and
Bill Clinton is getting ready to move over,
because you are destined to be king!

Well, I guess that this discourse ought to reach a logical and defensible conclusion. There is no question in my mind that the path to power comes as a consequence of pasture time, requiring that you follow God when you can't see Him, and that you never forget your brothers and sisters and prepare yourself for the giant. All of this, however, is still not sufficient to gain the power that you need. But this is what the text says:

Then Samuel took the horn of oil,
and anointed him in the midst of his brethren:
and the spirit of the Lord came upon David
from that day forward. (1 Samuel 16:13)

The Spirit of the Lord. That's the path. The Spirit of the Lord. Whatever you're going to do, what you need is the Spirit of the Lord. Whatever you're going to be, what you need is the Spirit of the Lord.

Whether you're in the pasture or in the palace, what you need is the Spirit of the Lord.

Whether you're in Morehouse or the White House, what you need is the Spirit of the Lord.

May I take just one minute to preach in here?

When the Spirit of the Lord is upon you something strange happens.

When the Spirit of the Lord is upon you, you'll feel things you never felt before.

When the Spirit of the Lord is upon you, you'll have power that you never had before.

When the Spirit of the Lord is upon you, you'll say things you never said before.

When the Spirit of the Lord is upon you, you'll stand up like David and say:

The Lord is my shepherd, I shall not want. (Psalm 23:1)

The Lord is my light and my salvation, whom shall I fear;
The Lord is the strength of my life, of whom shall I be afraid.
(Psalm 27:1)

I will lift up mine eyes unto the hills, from whence cometh my
help. My help cometh from the Lord, which made heaven and
earth. (Psalm 121:1-2)

I will bless the Lord at all times,
His praise shall continually be in my mouth.

My soul shall make her boast in the Lord,
the humble shall hear thereof and be glad.
Oh, magnify the Lord with me
and let us exalt his name together. (Psalm 34:1-3)

Wait on the Lord and be of good courage
and he shall strengthen thine heart.
Wait, I say, on the Lord. (Psalm 27:14)

❧ IV ❧
Policy Statements

CHAPTER THIRTEEN

From These Ashes!

The Washington Post
Outlook Editorial
June 23, 1996

The epidemic of fire and hatred against African American churches which has brought pain and outrage within the whole of the nation is a clear indication that we are still a nation divided, separate and unequal. The passionate hatred and violence of the 60's is yet with us; the stain of bigotry and racism still marks the collective soul and psyche of America. The thoughtful among us will agree that the pattern of arson against African American churches is reprehensible. That those who have planned or participated in what appears to be racially motivated and targeted acts of terrorism must be caught and punished is a foregone conclusion. Not since the bombing of the Sixteenth Street Baptist Church in Birmingham, Alabama in 1963 has there been such targeted violence against the Black Church. While some would suggest that these acts are not necessarily racially motivated, or that they are but the random violence of disturbed individuals, any such attempt at exoneration flies in the face of more compelling realities.

Ours is an era of *postmodern* thinking. We are told that there is no longer a belief in what is called a *Master Narrative*. Where once we shared standards and values which were not up for discussion, this is clearly no longer the case. In the 1990's we are told that no longer is there anything *true* and *real* in which we believe. The postmodern sensibility says that there are individual narratives but nothing is normative. We witness increasing materialism, the disappearance of connection to anything spiritual and an absence of common decency. It is this climate of relativism that has produced these acts of sinister violence.

But those who sought to destroy the African American church have instead underscored its significance and power. We might even suggest that those who are responsible for these burnings have greater appreciation for the significance of the African American church than those of us who are intimately involved in it. There is no doubt that the African American church is the most significant and powerful institution within our community. It is in the church that our leaders are born, our orators find their voice, and the center of our struggle is framed and forged. The church is the center of our struggle and our hope. One seeking to destroy the civil rights achievements of the last quarter century or the political and spiritual motivation of black people would certainly begin with an assault on the African American church. The burnings speak loudly and clearly: social programs will be scrapped, affirmative action is a thing of the past, scholarships will end, and Congressional districts will be redrawn. The message to African Americans is to *stay in your place.*

Following the national election of November 1994, a *USA Today* headline read: *"Angry White Men Get Their Revenge."* [25] The message was clear that in America one could now move against blacks with impunity. Newt Gingrich's Contract on America and Rush Limbaugh's reactionary ranting are an open invitation to rip open the ugly scars of America's racist past. Conservative Republicanism has borne its fruit.

The cross no longer burns in our yards; the cross burns at the place of our worship. Those who burn our churches know that if they can keep us out of the church they can keep us out of the ballot box. If they can burn us out of the church, they can burn us out of the bank. If they burn us out of the church, they can burn us out of schools and colleges. If they can burn us out of the church, they can burn out our opportunities for economic development and personal empowerment.

The fire which rages around the church rages as well in the soul of America. Consider the irony of recent history. The news is full of whites who are enraged about perceived injustices of our system of government. Skinheads, the Klan and the Aryan Faction have become an acceptable part of the social order. The standoff at Waco resulted in a fiery hell for the Branch Davidians; the crisis at

---

[25] *USA Today,* November 4, 1994.

Ruby Ridge occurred because of disenchanted persons seeking to secede from the government. African Americans do not seek to secede from the government. We are, by and large, God-fearing and patriotic. Yet, war has been declared on us. Must we now turn our thoughts toward protecting not only our churches but our homes and our schools? How far will this insanity go? Have we reached that era which the *Declaration of Independence* defined as "a long train of abuses and usurpations?" Is now the moment when we must "provide new guards for [our] future security?" We must be forever vigilant.

But our response must move beyond protection to power. The church has always been on fire. The church was born in fire and persecution. So shall it ever be. We must take from these ashes a determination to protect the institution as well as the people it serves. We must take from these ashes a determination to do for ourselves what the culture which surrounds us will never do. From these ashes we will restore the African American Church physically and spiritually, and make of it more than ever, a place of spiritual empowerment, political struggle, and economic development. From these ashes we will no longer be lulled to sleep by false beliefs that because a few have jobs or a few have degrees that the struggle is over and all is well. From these ashes will come a church that will no longer be content to let our children raise themselves, accept gang violence, or allow our women to suffer abuse and death at the hands of our men. The fire that burns around us cannot be compared with the fire that burns within us. From these ashes will come a people determined to be free.

CHAPTER FOURTEEN

Testimony on
Bill 12-280

❧

City Council of the District of Columbia
Law Enforcement Officer
Protection Act of 1997

To the Honorable Jack Evans, I am H. Beecher Hicks, Jr., Minister of Metropolitan Baptist Church in the District of Columbia. Ordinarily I would say that I am happy to testify before the Committee on the Judiciary, but today I am not. I am truly saddened by the events which make this occasion necessary, but at the same time, I am unalterably opposed to Bill 12-280.

Let it be clear that I share the broken heart of the entire community because of the recent deaths of three District of Columbia police officers and the suffering of their families. More to the point, I am extremely sympathetic to the family and friends of anyone who is slain. The nature of my ministry causes me to be in a caring relationship with all who know the anguish of unredemptive grief. My job is to walk weekly to the cemetery, there to bury the sad remains of this social insanity. Even within that context, however, my position against the death penalty is a longstanding one, a position which I trust will be taken seriously in this significant body.

In 1992 Congress tried to impose the death penalty on the District of Columbia. With the late D. C. City Council Chairman Dave Clarke, the Reverend Al Gallmon and I organized area ministers against the manufacturers of semi-automatic weapons. Our group was responsible for the *THOU SHALT NOT KILL* posters that were visible throughout the District. With the help of other groups, five years ago we mounted a citywide campaign to impose economic consequences upon the manufacturers of the weapons of death that caused blood to run in the streets of our city, and won by an overwhelming majority.

It is a strange and curious circumstance which leads us to discussing the death penalty before this committee. It is a strange and curious philosophy which posits that by killing killers we shall stop killing—that one act of savagery justifies another. Jesus of Nazareth, a Palestinian Preacher who was Himself publically murdered, suggested that civilized people cannot live by the philosophy of *an eye for an eye and a tooth for a tooth.* To live by such a philosophy, of course, would leave all of us snaggle-toothed and blind.

The reasons for my opposition to the death penalty are as old as the Mosaic Torah and are the same in the instance of the death of a police officer or of a private citizen. The same injunction we placed throughout this community in 1992 is the same injunction which must be given today: *THOU SHALT NOT KILL.*

The entire discussion of the death penalty as a deterrent to murder fails to take into account the culture of violence which has given rise to the segment of our population which has no value for life. While regrettably three police officers have lost their lives, and some suggest that police are being deliberately targeted for death, other innocent persons in the larger populace have also lost their lives through drive-by shootings, gangland-style murders, and acts of domestic violence which have literally caused blood to run in the streets of this city. Is one death more important than the next? I think not. Is it important that any person who works in public safety be protected by the law? Of course. But so must we all. Does community participation in the sentencing process make capital punishment any less barbaric? Of course not. Is the move toward capital punishment an effort to achieve political expediency at the expense of abandoning the high moral ground which is ours by our ancestry and by birth? Of course it is.

I have come today to take the position that we must respond most forcefully to those conditions which occasion irrational thought and unthinkable behavior: joblessness, homelessness, drug addiction, hopelessness and a whole myriad of social diseases which affect this community and so many others throughout this land.

I am opposed to the death penalty because of the frailty of our humanity. All of us are fallible, none of us more perfect than the other. We do not have a perfect criminal justice system. We have only to remember cases of prisoners being released after years of incarceration because of DNA tests that prove them innocent. Recent allegations of tampering with evidence by criminal justice authorities make it difficult if not impossible to place total faith in a system operated by mere mortals and therefore subject to critical error. Capital punishment leaves no margin for error; its consequences are mortally severe.

You are aware of the typical arguments against capital punishment:

- There is no credible evidence that the death penalty deters crime.
- States that have death penalty laws do not have lower crime rates or murder rates than states without such laws.
- States that have abolished capital punishment, or instituted it, show no significant changes in either crime or murder rates.

Like it or not, in reality such laws will do nothing to protect citizens or communities from the acts of dangerous criminals.

The issue at hand, however, is far more compelling and enticing. All reasonable persons would argue for the most elaborate protection of those who protect us. Nevertheless, in states where death penalty laws have been imposed specifically for the murder of a police officer, there is no evidence that the killing of police officers occurs less frequently than in states which do not have such laws. In fact, according to the National Law Enforcement Officers' Memorial Fund, Texas ranked fourth in the nation in 1996 in the number of police officers killed; second in 1995; and third in 1994. According to Law Enforcement News, prior to the statistics above, from 1988 through 1993, Texas ranked number one in police killings. If a death penalty for killing police officers did deter such murders, the statistics would be less striking.

The unvarnished truth about the criminal justice system in America is that the death penalty has a disparate impact on African Americans. Since the revival of the death penalty in the mid-1970's, about half of those on death row at any given time are of African American descent. During 1996, of the 3,200 prisoners on death row, 40% were black, in a nation where African Americans are approximately 12% of the population. It is not that people of color commit more murders; it is that they are more often sentenced to death when they do.

Poor people are also far more likely to be given death sentences than those who can afford the high costs of private investigators, psychiatrists and expert criminal lawyers for their defense. Some observers have pointed out that the term *capital punishment* is ironic because *only those without capital get the punishment.*

I am unequivocally in favor of providing every possible tool for recognizing the special contributions and risks of police officers, including significant pay raises. I am in favor of life without parole, life without parole at hard labor, life without parole in solitary confinement, or any other punishment which is at least morally defensible. Nevertheless, I personally oppose the death penalty under any guise. I am here today not only as a representative of 6,000 members of the Metropolitan Baptist Church but as a Prophet of the Living God to remind you that to pass this law would violate the high moral standard that must characterize the actions of those who sit in these seats of power and authority. You must not do violence to your own integrity or abandon what is in keeping with whatever religious principle you hold sacred. Yours must be a posture of protection for all citizens. You must not be duped into a mere punitive response in those unfortunate cases which involved only a few.

That we face a moral crisis there is no doubt. But we cannot resolve a moral crisis by immoral means. Though we are faced with rampant pathology which establishes violence as an acceptable response to the smallest slight, we cannot justify responding to this madness with more violence. Even as we respond to insanity, as a society we must be sane and civil in dealing with the perpetrators of crime. The quality of mercy must not be strained. Let there be no equivocation in my position: THOU SHALL NOT KILL!

CHAPTER FIFTEEN

"Give Me Liberty!"

Adapted by The Washington Post
Outlook Editorial *August 17, 1997*

The rapidly escalating controversy over the future of the District government, as well as the shifting power within it, provides the imperative for a word from a hitherto silent religious community. While I do not presume to speak for the entirety of that community, it is time for the church to be heard.

There can be no debate that the District government was, and yet remains, in serious disarray. It was reasonable that a serious effort be made to right the District's ship and set its sail on a new course of efficient delivery of public works and social services, as well as fiscal accountability and responsibility. What is most appalling, however, is that only now is the voice of serious protest being heard. That the citizens of the District—according to an inconclusive *Washington Post* poll—have indicated their indifference to these recent occurrences is equally alarming. It appears that the citizens of the city have been so focused on the reality of their present pain that they are quite willing to ignore the long term effects of this malignancy which is now upon us. That the ultimate takeover of the government and the dissolution of the powers of the Mayor and the City Council would be the inescapable result was patently clear from the first mention of the creation of a Control Board for the District. Now, however, for sides to rail at each other with racial rhetoric, or to believe that change will come by the use of '60s style demonstrations and such, is inappropriate and will gain little positive result.

We are aware that the Federal City is different in terms of the constitutional guarantees which permit the Congress to act, as it has, with impunity with respect to its management. To suggest, however, that the District government has been "all wrong" while the federal government has been "all right" is the highest form of public hypocrisy. It is clear to even those most sanguine among us that the District is in its condition not only because of internal political choices and mistakes but because the federal payment has been historically inconsistent and insufficient.

While the end the Congress seeks through the Control Board may prove to be right in the long term, the means by which it is achieved in the short term is specious at best. The maxim needed is not that "the end justifies the means" but rather, "two wrongs do not make a right." For Representative Davis to suggest that the Control Board was needed in order to save the city from "sliding into oblivion," causes me to suggest that in the end, this instant salvific process will be ultimately damnable. While the District is different from any other city in America, its people are not. The citizens of the District have every right to expect representative and participatory democracy in what is clearly the capital of democracy itself.

What we have here is not a civil rights issue, it is a human rights issue. This is not a simple matter of white over black, even though there is an unmistakable aura of a plantation mentality where all the decisions are made in the "Big House" and only a few chosen from the many are put in place to keep the "field workers" in check. This is not even a religious issue—it is about the consistent definition and exercise of time honored principles: freedom, democracy, honesty and integrity. We must move beyond any temptation to racial rhetoric to a far more important dialogue regarding the ethics of politics and our role in it. We must, if the District is to survive, come to an agreement not only regarding what we must demand but more importantly what we must value.

Rightly conceived, the Control Board should enable the citizens of the District to achieve their goals of independence and self-sufficiency. It should not interfere with the fundamental tenets of the very democracy which insures our freedoms. We can only blame ourselves for the inertia, the apathy, the failure to vote and for what the District by mismanagement and indolence has become; nevertheless, our children will also blame us if we do not fight to the death for the liberties which have been placed in serious peril by recent actions of the Congress and the President.

Many names are central to this conflict. We know them too well: Barry, Norton, Davis, Brimmer, Faircloth, Becton and the rest. We are in danger, I fear, of raising each of them to the level of "icon," there to become vilified either as the source of our shame or deified as the harbinger of our salvation. Far better we should insure that our debate does not center on these persons. If we have learned the lessons of history it is that we can no longer afford to sacrilize the persons and, in so doing, sacrifice the larger process. It is because we have historically placed such persons on precarious pedestals of public notoriety that we shamefully desecrate the rights of the people to govern themselves.

The Nation's Capital must be the showcase for the democratic process, and not an example of the enshrinement of colonialism, imperialism or miscellaneous dictatorial policies and practices, no matter how benevolent their supposed intent. While we are putting new roofs on our schools, we have sprung a leak at the very foundation stone of our democracy. What lessons shall we teach in our schools about the right, the purpose and the power of the vote? Which page of the government text book do we tear out when it comes to the issue of "taxation without representation"? Why should men and women of substance run for elected office in the District when those offices have been denuded of any vestige of power and authority? Sadly, the commentary of our time will be that in the democratic capital of the world the Mayor is in charge of playgrounds and the City Council is in frantic search for a meaningful agenda. It is time for saner, wiser heads to prevail.

Perhaps there are some positive suggestions to be made: First, if the Control Board is indeed an "emergency step" then let us be engaged in the process of planning now for the second step. The President should appoint a commission to oversee the reinstitution of "Home Rule" in the District and the restoration of all lost democratic powers for its people, and guarantee to the citizens of the District that this reinvestiture of democratic power will, in fact, occur. If this is not an "emergency step" but merely a Trojan horse used to cover what is intended to be a permanent reality, the ruse will be exposed and the battle rightfully joined.

Second, a leadership round table composed of a cross section of the city's leadership should be engaged in a continuing discussion aimed toward improvement at every level of city services. We cannot sacrifice the management of our city to the policies devised by paid consultants. (The notion that "consultants" shall become our saviors is curious indeed!) We must develop a new long-range plan which has the fingerprints of citizens from every walk of life all over it. Those who are stakeholders in this city must participate in a collaborative process which has purpose and meaning. In this connection, revenue and resources must be identified for the reinstitution of the city's Youth Leadership Program. We must consciously create within the District a generation of youth who will be nurtured and mentored to become the leaders this city will so desperately need in years to come. The children are our future. We can only depend on them to lead the way.

Third, the President must mandate that the Control Board put in place those initiatives which will insure economic development and the growth of minority enterprise, the highest quality of education for our children, improved public housing, responsibly supported social services and a determination that the quality of life in the District of Columbia will be maintained at the highest possible level.

Fourth, on those issues which exceed an expenditure of $10 million, the Control Board would place the issue at public referendum before the people to gain the advisory counsel and consent of the governed. Such a referendum would be achieved though computerized "kiosks" throughout the city, perhaps in grocery stores and gas stations, where persons by the press of a button could express their views on a particular issue for a period of one week. The result of the referendum would not be binding on the Control Board but would establish a clear mechanism for the people of this city to participate in their government while at the same time providing a mechanism through which the Control Board would itself be controlled.

Fifth, the Congress and the President should establish at once the privilege of a meaningful vote for the Delegate from the District to the House of Representatives.

Dismiss my sophomoric suggestions if you must, but at least let us reframe the discussion so that something positive can come from this very negative situation.

In 1775, days before the signing of the Declaration of Independence, Patrick Henry (his personal politics aside) spoke before the Virginia Provincial Convention and declared: "Is life so dear or peace so sweet as to be purchased by chains and slavery? Forbid it, Almighty God. I know not what course others may take but, as for me, give me liberty or give me death." Now, as then, the question of freedom and independence and sovereignty are uppermost in our minds. Anything less than liberty is unacceptable.